WILL THERE BE A TOMORROW?

Once the prophets of doom were pulpiteers. Now they are everywhere:

"Overpopulation will kill us all."

"Pollution will soon make our world uninhabitable."

"Worldwide famine and mass starvation are inevitable."

"It is already too late to save humanity."

Tomorrow? The world seems less and less sure that there will *be* a tomorrow. But the Bible teaches that the end is not yet. For the last act has not yet been played out on the stage of history.

What's left? What more can we expect? And why should we believe ancient biblical prophecies anyhow? This book may not answer those questions fully, but it will almost certainly give you more answers than you have now.

The author, Dr. Charles C. Ryrie, is professor of Systematic Theology, Dallas Theological Seminary. A Phi Beta Kappa member at Haverford College (A.B., 1946), he graduated with high honors from Dallas Theological Seminary (Th.D., 1949), and earned his Ph.D. (1954) from the University of Edinburgh. He has made several trips abroad, visiting, among other places, the Holy Land. He is the author of many books, including *Balancing the Christian Life, A Survey of Bible Doctrine,* and *Acts of the Apostles.* He is best known for the *Ryrie Study Bible.*

The Final Countdown

Originally titled *The Bible and Tomorrow's News*.
Revised and updated.

Charles C. Ryrie

This book is designed both for the reader's personal enjoyment and edification and for group study. A leader's guide is available from your local Christian bookstore or from the publisher.

VICTOR BOOKS ®

A DIVISION OF SCRIPTURE PRESS PUBLICATIONS INC.
USA CANADA ENGLAND

6 7 8 9 10 Printing/Year 94 93 92 91

Bible quotations are from the *King James Version*.

Recommended Dewey Decimal Classification: 236
  Suggested Subject Headings: PROPHECY, ESCHATOLOGY, SECOND ADVENT

Library of Congress Catalog Card Number: 81-52899
ISBN: 0-88207-347-8

VICTOR BOOKS
A division of SP Publications, Inc.
        Wheaton, Illinois 60187

CONTENTS

PREFACE

Prophecy seems to suffer at the hands of both its friends and foes. Friends sometimes overspeculate so that biblical passages are made to say more than they actually do; and foes overgeneralize so that the same passages are reduced to saying practically nothing.

Bible prophecy is a major area of biblical revelation, and we must seek to understand what the Bible is saying for itself. Reading in the spectacular and the contemporary is no better than reading out the clear and specific.

Undoubtedly events of recent decades have aroused an increasing interest in prophecy on the part of many people. Not only the establishment of the nation Israel in 1948 but the prominent place it continues to occupy in international diplomacy is inexplicable apart from an understanding of biblical prophecy. The economic interdependence of nations becomes more pronounced all the time. The ramifications of military action anywhere stagger our imagination and make many of us afraid of what might happen next.

In this book I try to present the biblical outline of things to come sanely, soberly, and truthfully. The framework is that of pretribulational premillennialism, though other positions are explained. I have tried to include all the major areas of prophecy, hoping that the discussion will not only increase the reader's knowledge, but also His love for the Lord who is the deliverer from the wrath to come.

A Look at Tomorrow

Almost everyone has some interest in prophecy. Millions read the daily horoscope in the newspaper. You may even have caught yourself stealing a glance at one, half believing that it could tell you how the day would turn out. Astrology and fortune-telling are big businesses today.

The unstable political climate worldwide also generates an interest in prophecy. Government leaders demonstrate all too often that they do not have the answers. Many seem to realize more than ever today that the Bible has something reliable to say about tomorrow's headlines. And, in fact, it is the only accurate source of information about the future.

Why Study Prophecy?

All of the Bible is profitable and practical (2 Tim. 3:16-17). Prophecy seems to be especially important for a number of good reasons:

1. *Understanding prophecy produces poise in a person.* Poise is defined as balance and stability. But how can anyone be stable in a world like ours? A dog-eat-dog attitude pervades business affairs. The materialism of this day of plenty puts pressure on all of us. Increased income has brought increased spending and greater pressures. Unrest in our cities and rebellion against authority make people afraid to walk the streets. Parents are afraid for their children, races fight each other, and nations compete in the nuclear arms race. In the church, apostasy, indifference, and deadness are common. False intellectualism is so rampant that we are told that the unbelievers are the real believers, and that God is, for all practical purposes, useless.

We cannot help but wonder where the trend will lead. Has the church any message for this confused day? Can a Christian be poised when everyone else seems completely unbalanced? The answers to these questions are in the Bible and particularly found in understanding God's program for the future. Seeking to understand biblical truths will impart a certainty and confidence not available elsewhere.

Can we really be *certain* about what prophecy teaches us? There are "prophecy quacks" who abuse and pervert the truth. There are others who say we should not study prophecy at all. Both these attitudes are dangerous. It is obviously wrong to pervert the truth, but it is equally bad to ignore it. Therefore, we ought to be careful students of prophecy. No one refuses to use money simply because some counterfeit money is being circulated! Actually, the presence of false currency makes us more careful in handling what is genuine, and one learns to be on guard against the counterfeit by accurate knowledge of the real thing. It is much the same with prophecy.

The Apostle Paul followed such a plan when false teachers at Thessalonica began to teach that the Day of the Lord had already come (2 Thes. 2:2). To counteract this teaching, Paul simply explained to the Thessalonians again the truth about the matter. Paul thought the average believer could and should know the details of prophecy. He did not want Christians to be ignorant of the truth nor to hold a false view of it. He wanted them to be *certain* so their attitude would reflect the confidence and poise that becomes Christians, even in a confused age.

2. *An understanding of prophecy brings comfort in the face of sorrow*. What believer stands in front of an open grave without thinking of the certainty of the resurrection of the body? Or who, when misunderstood or wronged, has not thought ahead to the time when the Lord will come and "bring to light the hidden things of darkness, . . . and then shall every man have praise of God" (1 Cor. 4:5)? We often take prophetic truths for granted, but can you imagine how hopelessly insecure and frustrated you would be, when

confronted with such situations, if you did not *know* something about the future? Many early Christians, converted out of heathenism, were ignorant concerning Christian teachings. Merely learning, for the first time, what happens after death must have revolutionized their outlook.

Today we live in a culture in which the Bible has been available for centuries. It is impossible for us to imagine the effect of a passage like 1 Thessalonians 4:13-18 as it was first read by early Christians. What did it mean to them that the dead in Christ will be raised with new bodies when the Lord comes? Think of the excitement of knowing that living believers may never see death but could be changed instantly at the return of Christ!

Up to that time, all that the Greek and Roman civilizations told men about death was contained in such descriptive terms as "bitter," "ruinous," "relentless," "the eternal chamber of those who have withered," and "among the living, hope endures, but hopeless are the dead." The certainty of the Christian message brings comfort—comfort that is found in the prophetic portions of the Word of God.

3. *God considers prophecy important*. What other conclusion can you reach? About one fourth of the Bible, when it was written, was unfulfilled prophecy. Whole books, in both the Old and New Testaments (Zechariah, 1 Thessalonians, and Revelation), are devoted to prophecy. If *God* gives so much attention to the subject, we should not neglect it—but we do neglect and abuse it.

Anything important and worthwhile usually involves dangers, and there are dangers in the study of prophecy. One danger is the spirit of Athenianism.

You remember that the Athenians delighted to hear "some new thing" (Acts 17:21). Unfortunately, some people today study prophecy in that spirit, and the result is spiritual pride. They take pride in knowing all the fine distinctions between the first beast and the second beast, or the king of the north as contrasted with the king of the south. Such pride is a real danger in studying prophecy.

Sometimes, too, people make this important subject a false basis for Christian fellowship. Our fellowship is basically in Christ, not in some particular view of prophecy. It's true that one may have closer fellowship with those who hold similar views on prophecy and the other doctrines of the Bible, but it is not right to deny fellowship on this basis.

A third danger is to study prophecy simply to satisfy curiosity. This large portion of the Bible is not to be examined and studied as if it were a curiosity piece that intrigues for a while but is soon discarded. The importance of prophecy lies not only in the facts it teaches but in the way it affects our daily living.

In spite of these dangers, we must not minimize the importance of biblical prophecy.

4. *Prophecy is a great tool for the conviction and conversion of unbelievers*. Frequently preachers of the New Testament had this end in view in their use of certain facts about the future. In the first weeks of the church's existence, Peter preached a sermon which is almost entirely prophetic (Acts 3:12-26). Regardless of how the full meaning and intent of his words concerning the kingdom are interpreted, this prophetic message convicted and converted many hearers.

James referred to an Old Testament prophecy when deciding the matters that came before the Jerusalem Council (Acts 15:16-17). Paul preached the details of prophecy to the Thessalonians during his brief stay in that city (Acts 17:2; 2 Thes. 2:5). Shortly afterward, in Athens, he spoke of coming judgment; as a result many were convicted and a few converted (Acts 17:31-34). When he said farewell to the Ephesian elders, he told them that he had not "shunned to declare . . . all the counsel of God" (Acts 20:27), which must have included prophecy. In the last glimpse we have of Paul, he was in Rome "preaching the kingdom of God, and teaching those things which concern the Lord Jesus Christ" (Acts 28:31).

Preachers and people have been doing the same throughout the years. Explaining and warning about the future should be an important part of any witness or ministry. When our Lord told His disciples about the ministry the Holy Spirit would have in bringing conviction to the hearts of men in this age, He said this work of conviction would involve three things: sin, righteousness, and judgment (John 16:7-11). "Judgment" refers to the future judgment that will come on all unbelievers. The positive proof that it will certainly come is the fact that Satan has already *been* judged (John 12:31; 16:11). In other words, if Satan has not escaped judgment, how can anyone who persists in rejecting Jesus Christ as Saviour expect to escape? Here Paul used a future event to convict and convert men.

You may be able to use *your* knowledge of prophecy this way! Share with someone what you learn in this study. Take your neighbor to hear a message on prophecy or to see pictures of Palestine. The message of prophecy may bring conviction and possibly conversion.

5. *The study of prophecy should bring cleansing to the one studying.* "Every man that hath this hope in Him purifieth himself, even as [Christ] is pure" (1 John 3:3). Unfortunately, in the confusion of these times, some Christians, knowing that the end may be near, occasionally throw up their hands and abandon themselves to whatever immediate "pleasure" they can get out of life. Instead, knowledge of the nearness of Christ's return should motivate each Christian to live each day as if it were his last.

Regrettably, a speaker or writer occasionally misuses the truth that today may be the day the Lord is coming. He will use this truth as a sort of club to beat God's people into right living. This approach is wrong because it puts a premium on the day of Christ's return, as if that day were more important than any other day. The Bible gives no such special prominence to the day or the moment of the Lord's return. Actually, each day of our lives is equally important, for when the Lord comes He will not simply review the *last day,* but *every* day of our Christian experience.

The cleansing hope that the Lord's return ought to bring to a believer's life is illustrated by the Nazarite vow in the Old Testament. A Nazarite was one who took a special vow to separate himself to the Lord (Num. 6:2). Actually, the word "Nazarite" means *to separate,* and a Nazarite was a separatist in the best sense of that word. He showed his separation in various ways. He abstained from certain luxuries which others were permitted to enjoy. He avoided contact with dead bodies as a symbol of his separation from sin. In other words, the Nazarite vowed to live an especially godly life of separation to God.

The Greek word for "purify" (1 John 3:3) is the term commonly used in the Greek Old Testament in connection with the Nazarite vow. Seeing what was involved in a Nazarite vow gives us a vivid illustration of how a New Testament believer should be cleansed in the hope of Christ's coming. Could it be that the present lack of preaching, teaching, and study of prophecy in many churches is a reason why today's standard of spirituality is so low? Almost without exception, the mention of the coming of Christ in the New Testament is followed by an exhortation to godliness.

6. *Knowledge of the future should breed consistency throughout one's life*. The Apostle Paul stated this sixth and culminating benefit of the study of prophecy at the conclusion of one of his discussions concerning the future: "Therefore, my beloved brethren, be ye steadfast, unmoveable, always abounding in the work of the Lord, forasmuch as ye know that your labor is not in vain in the Lord" (1 Cor. 15:58). The principal thrust of this exhortation is toward "abounding in the work of the Lord." The words *steadfast, unmoveable*, and *always* show clearly that such labors are not to be spasmodic or lacking in continuity. No "off again, on again" kind of Christian living and witness is permitted.

We have seen that God does not place a premium on the last day or last moment before Christ's return. God expects consistent living *every* day, especially in those who know something about prophecy. Actually, our knowledge of the future affects the present in various ways as the following examples illustrate.

Monday was always washday in the home where I grew up. We collected all the soiled clothes in a pile at the head of the stairs Sunday night as we prepared to go to bed. The knowledge of what was going to happen on Monday guided our actions on Sunday night.

If you follow basketball or football, you know how closely coaches and players look at the clock as time begins to run out in a game. Often it's time for new plays, special strategy. So it should be with a Christian—the knowledge of God's timetable, as gained through the study of prophecy, should affect his activity every day.

Consider these six reasons for studying prophecy: to give confidence in the face of perplexities, to bring comfort in sorrow, to grow in understanding one fourth of the Bible, to use in the conviction and conversion of unbelievers, and to cleanse and bring consistency to your life.

What Is Prophecy?

The dictionary says that prophecy is a declaration of something to come, or a prediction. When we apply this definition to the prophecies of the Bible, we realize immediately that where we stand in history will determine what we consider to be prophecy. Strictly speaking, prophecy is the foretelling of anything that is future.

The Bible contains many prophecies which have already been fulfilled and are now history. But there are many Bible prophecies still to be fulfilled, and we expect them to come to pass exactly as predicted. In this book, we will focus attention on the prophecies to be fulfilled—the ones which will make tomorrow's headlines.

Christ's Promise about Prophecy

Before our Lord was crucified, He made a prediction and gave a promise to His disciples. He told them that "when He, the Spirit of truth, is come, He will guide you into all truth . . . and He will show you things to come" (John 16:13). A little earlier, Jesus had said that it was necessary for Him to put off telling the disciples some things, while He was on earth, simply because they could not understand them until after His resurrection and the coming of the Holy Spirit.

The Holy Spirit is here now, to guide Christians into all truth. This includes knowledge of Christ Himself (for He *is* the Truth) and of all things revealed in the Word of God. But particularly, the Spirit will show believers "things to come." We are specifically promised help in the study of prophecy, and that promise ought to be a great encouragement as you study this subject. Think of all the specific items on the curriculum of Christian truth that Jesus might have mentioned in connection with the Spirit's teaching ministry! He called attention to only *one*—prophecy. It is almost as if the Lord anticipated the reluctance with which some believers would approach this subject and so gave this encouraging promise. It is the Holy Spirit Himself, the divine Author of the Bible, who will guide our look at tomorrow. With a promise like this, we ought to be all the more challenged to thoroughly investigate the prophecies of God's Word.

Ground Rules for Prophecy Study

"But," some will say, "isn't the language of prophecy full of symbols? And doesn't this fact make it practically impossible for us to understand prophecy?" The answer to these questions is found in the basic relationship between communication and language. Language is God's gift to man. God planned it so that language would be fully capable of communicating to man all that God wanted to say. In the Bible, God communicates His message to us in language that conveys truth. In other words, God is *revealing* things to us in the Bible, not *hiding* things from us. This is true of the prophetic portions as well as other passages.

If the Bible conveys actual or literal truth from God, it follows that the Bible ought to be interpreted literally. And this is the first and all-important ground rule for studying prophecy—interpret *literally*. Some people do not like the word "literal," since it seems to preclude anything symbolic. Perhaps the word "plain" (or "normal") would be better than "literal," for we recognize that the Bible *does* use symbols and figures of speech in the process of conveying literal truth. However, in recognizing this we are *not* saying that the Bible should be interpreted *symbolically*; rather we are saying that its symbols and figures of speech must be translated into literal truth in order for us to clearly understand the message God wants to convey.

"But," you may say, "how can a symbol be interpreted literally?" Actually how else could it be understood? If a symbol does not represent an actual or *literal* truth, then it must be a symbol of another *symbol*, and the process goes on and on and becomes completely meaningless. Somewhere along the line, a symbol *must* represent something *literal*. That is why we insist that symbols and figures of speech must be understood plainly. There is no alternative.

Take Psalm 22 as an example. In verses 12 and 13, the intense hatred of Christ's enemies is likened to bulls of Bashan and to a ravening and roaring lion. Behind these symbols stand certain literal facts which give meaning to the symbols. The bulls of Bashan were an exceptionally fine breed known for their strength (Deut. 32:14; Ezek. 39:18), and the ferocity of lions is proverbial. The strength and fierceness of Christ's adversaries are vividly described by the use of these symbols—they make the meaning of the passage *more* plain.

But what about Revelation? It is full of symbols, and it plays a large part in a study of prophecy. Can we interpret it literally? The answer must be yes, for we must interpret it in the same manner as we interpret the rest of the Bible. If it uses symbols and figures of speech, they must convey *literal* truth in order to have meaning. Take, as an example, Revelation 8:12 and 9:1-2. In 8:12, a judgment is prophesied which will affect the sun, moon, stars, day, and night. The stars referred to in this verse are undoubtedly the astronomical bodies in the heavens, which we would call literal stars. But in chapter 9:1-2, John records the fact that he saw a star fall from heaven to whom was given the key of the pit, and that this star opened the pit. This star must be a symbol representing some created being (probably an angel) who performs these acts. In English, we use the word "star" in the same two ways. We speak of the "stars" in the skies above—literal astronomical bodies. But we also refer to the "stars" of an athletic contest, and in this case we mean human beings. The *symbol* has meaning simply because people can shine or stand out or sparkle as literal stars do. Use of the symbol heightens the literal meaning of our statement.

To be sure, there may be times when we do not understand the meaning of a symbol—or even of a plain statement. In such cases we should not devise a symbolic interpretation; rather, we should continue to search for the literal truth that God is trying to convey through the statement. Straightforward, plain, normal, literal interpretation is the most basic of all guidelines for the study of prophecy.

A second ground rule for interpreting prophecy is this: compare one prophecy with another. This principle was stated by Peter: "Knowing this first, that no prophecy of the Scripture is of any private interpretation" (2 Peter 1:20). In other words, no prophecy is to be interpreted by itself, but in the light of all that God has spoken on the subject. Every prophecy is *part* of the *total* picture. No single prophet received the entire picture; rather, the plan unfolds piece by piece, without contradiction, to reveal the complete and perfect picture. If difficulties of interpretation arise, they are not contradictions, for the Bible is a harmonious and consistent whole.

A third guideline is this: remember that sometimes future events are so mingled together in a prophecy that they seem to be peaks in a range of mountains, the valleys being hidden. In other words, sometimes two future events are predicted one right after the other, but their fulfillment may be separated by many years (or centuries). For example, often events connected with the first and second comings of Christ are found in the writings of the same prophet, even though their fulfillment has already been separated by nearly 2,000 years (Isa. 9:6-8; 61:1-2). All the predicted events either have been or will be fulfilled literally, even though the prophet may not have seen the time gaps involved between their fulfillments.

A fourth similar principle is sometimes called the law of double reference. It simply means that a prophecy may have a double fulfillment—one in the immediate circumstances and time of the prophet, and another in the distant future. Isaiah 7:14 is an example.

Apparently some child born in the time of Ahaz was a sign to him, and yet this great prophecy was not completely fulfilled until Christ was born. Often God used this principle, giving both a near and far view in the same prophecy, so that the fulfillment of the one would be assurance of the fulfillment of the other. But notice again, both near and far fulfillments are *literal*. *Literal interpretation* is the key to understanding all the Bible, including prophecy.

Remember the Promise

It's hard to imagine a more interesting time in which to study prophecy than today, with its rapid movement of events. We find the Bible mentions those events that will make tomorrow's headlines. The study of prophecy gives poise and confidence in the face of confusion; it brings comfort in sorrow; it must not be neglected because one fourth of the Bible was prophetic when written; it can be used to bring conviction and conversion to bewildered people; and it ought to bring cleansing and consistency to your life. These are some of the reasons why we study prophecy.

In this book, we focus on predictions yet to be fulfilled. In understanding prophecy we must consistently follow literal interpretation. Even the symbols and figures of speech have plain meanings behind them.

If while reading and studying you begin to feel bogged down, remember the promise of Jesus, who assures us that the Holy Spirit will show us things to come. Try to understand all that you can; ask the Holy Spirit to show you the true meaning of these prophecies; be concerned with what you *do* understand. More and more will become clear as you study. And with the knowledge gained, you'll enjoy the practical benefits of knowing God's Word about tomorrow's news.

2
Empires Come and Go

It's the natural tendency of people to assume that *their* nation will continue forever. But empires come and go, and this generation has seen that very thing happen. Even the greatest of nations may sink into oblivion overnight, and new nations may emerge (as in Africa) with a rapidity that makes it hard to even learn their names.

All these changes of political fortune do not happen by chance. The events of history lie in the sovereign hands of God, who is actively carrying forward His plan for the world. He does not leave us in the dark about this plan, as we shall see in this chapter.

Have you ever heard a Christian say (usually with a heavy sigh of resignation), "Yes, I know that God is *still* on the throne!" One gets the impression that God is about to be toppled from His throne by whatever misfortune called forth the comment. The truth of the matter is that God is not only on His throne but is also actively, positively, and sovereignly controlling the affairs of men to suit His own purposes.

Daniel realized this truth and said, God "removeth kings and setteth up kings" (Dan. 2:21), and "He doeth according to His will in the army of heaven and among the inhabitants of the earth" (4:35). This was not a lesson that came easily to Daniel. He had been violently uprooted from his family and from his homeland by the ruthless conquest of Palestine by Nebuchadnezzar. Suddenly he found himself in a strange country under the rule of an absolute monarch whose authority was unchallenged and whose empire seemed permanent when Daniel spoke these words. But the Babylonian Empire *was* in time overthrown; other empires rose and fell. By the same token, the powerful nations of *our* day may not be the political forces of tomorrow. Indeed, the headlines of tomorrow's newspapers will scream the defeats of nations we know today.

Nebuchadnezzar's Dream

Daniel saw all this in the remarkable dream of Nebuchadnezzar, the king of Babylon. And his interpretation of Nebuchadnezzar's dream foretold the history of the kingdoms of the world.

As Nebuchadnezzar was thinking about the future one night (Dan. 2:29), God gave him a dream, which troubled him when he awoke. Nebuchadnezzar decided to use the dream to test the supposed wise men of his realm. Apparently he had not forgotten the dream ("The thing is gone from me," v. 3, should read, "The thing is certain to me"; note v. 9). He was puzzled by the dream's meaning. If he had told the wise men the dream, they could have made up an interpretation, but because they did not know the dream they could not fool the king. However, in answer to the united prayer of Daniel and his friends, God gave Daniel knowledge both of the dream and of its meaning.

In his dream, the king had seen a great image. "This great image, whose brightness was excellent, stood before thee," said Daniel, "and the form thereof was terrible" (v. 31). It was made up of four different metals. The head was gold; the breast and arms were silver; the belly and sides were brass; the legs, iron; and the feet, iron and clay. Then a stone struck the image at the feet and crushed it completely, breaking it into pieces, which the wind carried away. The stone became a mountain that filled the entire earth (v. 35). As Daniel revealed the dream, the king was undoubtedly nodding approval, for this was exactly what he had dreamed, and he was anxious to hear what was sure to be the correct interpretation of what he had seen.

Before looking at the particulars of the interpretation, we need to relate the subject of the dream to God's people, Israel. God had given Israel a title deed to Palestine, and had said that this land would always be hers. The Lord had promised King David that one of his sons would reign over the nation forever. But a strange thing had taken place. The nation that belonged in Palestine under the rule of a Davidic king was now in a foreign land under the rule of a foreign (or Gentile) king.

What had happened? God was chastening His people. Israel had sinned in worshiping idols and had been unfaithful to God. In Nebuchadnezzar's dream, God was revealing who would reign over Israel from the time of the Babylonian captivity until Messiah would come to restore her land and her rightful king.

Daniel explained the various parts of the image:

1. *The Head* (vv. 37-38). The head of gold represented Nebuchadnezzar and his empire. The phrase, "Thou art this head of gold," does not refer personally to Nebuchadnezzar but to his kingdom. In other words, Babylon was the first world empire to rule over the Jews and their city Jerusalem.

At that time, the Babylonian Empire included much of civilized Asia, and the city of Babylon was at the zenith of its glory under Nebuchadnezzar's reign (605-562 B.C.). The city, about 14 miles square, included vast fortifications, famous streets, canals, temples, and palaces. Its hanging gardens were, to the Greeks, one of the seven wonders of the ancient world. It is not strange that Nebuchadnezzar boasted, "Is not this great Babylon, which I have built for the house of the kingdom by the might of my power and for the honor of my majesty?" (4:30) Undoubtedly the more than a million people who lived inside Babylon thought this empire would never fall. The walls of the capital city were 87 feet thick and 350 feet high. But Babylon *did* fall—not long after the death of Nebuchadnezzar. Four kings and 21 years later, the mighty kingdom came to a sudden end.

2. *The Breast and Arms* (v. 39). Saying "after thee" to Nebuchadnezzar was about like saying "after the United States has been conquered"—but it happened! On October 13, 539 B.C., Babylon was defeated by the Medes and the Persians, and from that

time on the city gradually fell into decay and ruin. All that Daniel's interpretation says about Medo-Persia, the second empire, is that it would be inferior to Babylon (as silver is inferior to gold). That inferiority was lack of inner unity—for the empire, after it succumbed to the Medes and Persians, was divided. This lack of unity was symbolized, in the image, by the progression from a single head to the breast and two arms (three parts). The Persian Empire flourished from 539-531 B.C.

3. *The Belly and Sides* (v. 39b). With the conquests of Alexander the Great, the Persian Empire was superseded by the Greek. All Daniel 2 says about Greece is that her sway would be worldwide in scope. Elsewhere Daniel predicts the division of the Greek Empire among Alexander's four generals (7:6—"four heads"; 8:21-22, where Greece is named; 11:2-4) after his death.

4. *The Legs and Feet* (vv. 40-43). The metals of the image—from gold to silver to brass and now to iron—indicate a decrease in quality but an increase in strength. One historian has said of it: "To resist it was fatal, and to flee was impossible." But in the toes we see another substance—clay. Daniel interprets this to mean more division, with resultant loss of unity and strength. In Daniel 7, a parallel vision, we learn more about the "10 toes" of the Roman Empire. All that we need to know about them now is that they represent 10 kings or a 10-kingdom form of the empire (7:24).

5. *The Stone* (vv. 44-45). The stone is Christ (see 7:9). His coming will destroy all the kingdoms of this world, and His kingdom will encompass the entire earth (2:35). The kingdom of Christ, as prophesied here, is related to *earth*, not heaven.

But when has this been, or when will it be? Obviously, at His first coming Christ did not even establish a kingdom in Palestine, to say nothing of the whole earth. Therefore we are forced to conclude that the kingdom will be set up at His Second Coming. A lot of confusion would be avoided if we would remember a very simple comparison: the first coming of Christ was related to the cross; the second, to the kingdom. This is confirmed in Daniel's interpretation of the dream.

He says that this kingdom will be set up "in the days of these kings" (2:44)—that is, in the days of the 10-kingdom form of the Roman Empire. Since Rome has not yet existed in this 10-kingdom form, the coming of the Stone must be future.

A Time Gap

As Daniel foresaw the sweep of human governments, both in his interpretation (chap. 2) and in his own vision (chap. 7), he saw the fourth empire, Rome, followed immediately by the coming of Christ and the setting up of His kingdom. But Rome came to an end, as a world power, hundreds of years ago—and Christ has not yet come. How do we explain this?

Here is one of those time gaps which we mentioned as a guideline for interpreting prophecy. The years between the decline of the Roman Empire and the establishing of its 10-kingdom form were not seen by Daniel but were simply passed over in these visions. It is as if Daniel saw only the mountain peak of the "leg" form of Rome at and after the first coming of Christ, and then another mountain peak of the "10 toes" form of Rome, and did not see the years in the valley between (figure 1).

Probably the clearest example of this principle is found in Isaiah 61:1-2, as quoted by the Lord (Luke 4:18-19). In the Nazareth synagogue, Jesus read Isaiah's prophecy as far as the middle of verse 2, where He stopped suddenly and said, "This day is this Scripture fulfilled in your ears." Why did He not quote Isaiah's entire

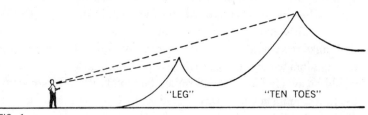

"LEG"   "TEN TOES"

FIG. 1

sentence? The answer can only be because the part He did not quote was not being fulfilled that day. It concerned the day of vengeance of God, which coincides with His second coming.

In other words, Isaiah saw events related to both advents of Christ in one profile of prophecy; Christ, knowing he would fulfill the two predictions at different times, separated those events which were fulfilled at His coming from those which await His return. Likewise, the 10-kingdom form of Rome awaits a future day for its fulfillment.

Tomorrow's Political Headlines

Since the 10-toes form of the Roman Empire is yet to come, we can expect that someday headlines will announce the formation of a confederation of 10 nations in the general area of the old Roman Empire—western Europe. In a parallel vision (Dan. 7), Daniel learned that the four beasts in that vision, corresponding to the four different metals in the image Nebuchadnezzar saw, represented the four world empires and that the fourth would "devour the whole earth . . . tread it down and break it in pieces" (7:23). Then the interpreter went on to say that the 10 horns (corresponding, evidently, to the 10 toes in the image) were 10 kings that will arise out of that fourth or Roman Empire (v. 24).

This is why we can say with certainty that such a federation will come into being *before* the Lord returns. Why *before?* Because the stone of chapter 2 smites the image on its feet, and the Ancient of Days (chap. 7) fights against this federation and is victorious over it. So the federation must be in existence, and functioning, at the Second Coming of Christ.

The federation will be formed in the early months of the tribulation period, just after the Lord has taken all believers (dead and living) to be with Him forever (1 Thes. 4:13-17). Apparently the political necessity for self-defense will prompt this union. There will be other great power blocs in the tribulation days, and the countries of western Europe would be unable to defend themselves if left to their individual efforts. They will realize the absolute necessity of pooling their resources, which will result in what we could call the Federated States of Europe.

But this is not all. Daniel also saw another little horn (7:8, 20-21, 24-26), who came from among the 10, was greater than the others, subdued 3 of the 10, blasphemed God, and persecuted the saints.

As the federation is forming, this man—who will become the great leader of the federation—will begin his startling rise to power. Since he is from among the 10 kings, he will evidently be from the area of the old Roman Empire. If Christ comes for His saints within, say, the next 30 years, this man is very likely already living. If the Lord is coming sooner, then this leader is probably already active in politics. His rise to power will be welcomed, since 10 sovereign nations will not combine their destinies and give up their sovereignty easily. A strong leader will be needed to prod them into federation. The "little horn" will supply this leadership, and his name and feats will often make headlines in the first part of the Tribulation.

Three times in these verses, we are told that this man must conquer 3 of the 10 nations. Presumably, not all the 10 countries are happy about losing their independence, so 3 resist efforts at union. Whether this will involve open war or whether it will be done by more indirect means, we do not know. But we *do* know that forcing the 3 nations into an involuntary federation will make headlines.

When this leader has consolidated his own political empire, he will, among other things, blaspheme God and persecute the people of God who are living during the Tribulation. His empire is sometimes called the revived Roman Empire because it is connected, in both the image and the vision, with Rome, the fourth great empire.

Even though believers of our age will have been taken to heaven before the Tribulation begins, some people will be converted during those awful days, and they (or perhaps the Jews) will be the people of God whom this man will persecute. But the persecution will not get out of control. God will be sovereign in those days, too. "They shall be given" (Dan. 7:25)—the passive voice—shows that God allows this persecution.

Notice, too, that the duration of the persecution is limited to "a time and times, and the dividing of time." This refers to the last half of the Tribulation period, or three and one half years $(1 + 2 + \frac{1}{2} = 3\frac{1}{2})$. This same persecution, during the same period of time, is described again in Revelation 12:13-17. Those living at that time, at least in western Europe, will see news reports of their leader's exploits in killing many of God's people.

Common Market and Antichrist

This western leader is such an important figure in the Tribulation days that we need to look at him a little more closely. Daniel calls him "the little horn" (7:8), "the prince that shall come" (9:26); and "the king [who] shall do according to his will" (11:36). Paul calls him "that man of sin" (2 Thes. 2:3), and John refers to him several times as "the beast" (Rev. 11:7; 13:1; 17:11; 19:20). In this study, we shall endeavor to use the title "man of sin," which will help us remember that he is a real human being ("man") whose chief aim is to oppose God ("of sin"). Indeed, many rightly call him the Antichrist (1 John 2:22).

Understanding that this man will be the great political ruler in the west is as far as we need to go in our study of him just now. He will also be active in religious matters and military campaigns, but we shall consider these later.

Is there any relation between current events and the future headlines that will feature the activities of the man of sin? Presumably there is, and it doesn't take much insight to realize this. The European Common Market *may* be the link between today's happenings and these events of the Tribulation days. With the Common Market has come a kind of union, at the moment more economic than political, which could lead to other and stronger ties between the countries in that group.

The reason we can only say that the Common Market *may* be the link is that no one can be sure if this is the organization on which will be built what will ultimately lead to the Federated States of Europe. It easily *could* be. But we must admit that the Common Market could dissolve completely and another organization could appear immediately, or after some lapse of time, which would turn out to be the forerunner of the Federation. We must also include the possibility that there will be *no* preliminary organization leading to the final form of the Federated States. A confederation could easily spring up overnight, without any prior organization.

We are becoming accustomed to fast-changing political alignments. Changes in power come overnight in Russia. In the Middle East, sworn enemies who, over their respective radios, were cursing the ground each other walked on, have been seen signing a mutual assistance pact the next day. Revolutions in Latin American countries change the government in a matter of hours. It is possible that the man of sin could form a federation in a very short time. But it is equally true that such organizations as the Common Market make it all the more easy, humanly speaking, for this to happen.

"The Times of the Gentiles"

The period of the rise and fall of Daniel's four great world empires, beginning with Babylon and ending with the fall of the 10-kingdom Roman federation at the Second Coming of Christ, is called "the times of the Gentiles." This term is found only once in the Bible: "And they shall fall by the edge of the sword, and shall be led away captive into all nations: and Jerusalem shall be trodden down of the Gentiles until the times of the Gentiles be fulfilled" (Luke 21:24).

Various meanings have been given to the phrase, but the correct one, it seems, must take into account the sign of the period mentioned in the verse: the city of Jerusalem shall be *trodden down*. The particular construction of the verb here gives the idea of a chronic condition, and this state of Jerusalem is the principal characteristic of the times of the Gentiles.

A similar phrase, "the fullness of the Gentiles," occurs in Romans 11:25. Again, various meanings have been assigned, but the context gives the right clue to the meaning of the term. Paul has been discussing the matter of spiritual blessing. He says the people of

Israel enjoyed that privilege first. Then, because of their unbelief, they were cut off and Gentiles were given the place of spiritual blessing. But once again God is going to bless Israel, so that all Israel will be saved (11:26). This will occur after the Tribulation, at the Second Coming of Christ. It will include, as the text says, *all* Jews living at that time.

This group of Jews, however, will have passed through the Tribulation *and* through a judgment at the end of that period that will purge out all rebels (Ezek. 20:37-38). Only those whose hearts have been judged right in God's sight will be saved, and that will be 100 percent of the group living at that particular moment. A spiritual blindness will be on Israel (the Jews) until the fullness of the Gentiles comes in (Rom. 11:25), or until the end of the time when Gentiles are being blessed.

This does not mean that Jews are not being saved today, but that God is calling people primarily from among Gentiles. For those of us who believe that the rapture of the church will occur before the Tribulation, the fullness of the Gentiles will come to an end at the Rapture. Then God will begin to judge Gentile nations, during the seven years of tribulation, and at the end of that time He will judge and redeem living Israelites. Thus the phrase "fullness of the Gentiles" relates to spiritual blessing, and "the times of the Gentiles" relates to the domination by Gentiles of a particular city.

When did the times of the Gentiles begin? Luke 21:24 does not say, though some believe it indicates that the beginning was in A.D. 70, when the Romans destroyed Jerusalem. However, most understand the beginning of the period to be the time when Nebuchadnezzar overran Jerusalem in 605 B.C., destroying the city and the temple and taking the Jews into captivity. Jerusalem was certainly trodden down at that time, the first instance of complete disruption of the commonwealth of Israel since its beginning. Notice how thoroughly Nebuchadnezzar devastated the city. His troops killed the young men, butchered women and old people mercilessly, took the precious vessels of the temple to Babylon, burned the temple itself, and carried the Jews into captivity (2 Chron. 36:17-20). Gentile Babylon trod down Jerusalem in a most decisive way. This view would make the beginning of the times of the Gentiles coincide with the beginning of the period marked off by the image about which Nebuchadnezzar dreamed. The head of gold—Nebuchadnezzar— was the first to be lord over Jerusalem.

When will the times of the Gentiles end? When Israel occupied Old Jerusalem and the temple area during the Six-Day War in June 1967, some thought this signaled the end of the period, for Jerusalem was no longer trodden down by the Gentiles. However, the Bible clearly states that Jerusalem will still be trodden down by the Gentiles during the Tribulation. Indeed, Revelation 11:2 is the only other place (besides Luke 21:24) where this verb for "trodden down" is used. To believe that the times of the Gentiles ended in 1967 would also necessitate believing that the "times" will resume in the Tribulation. Is there not a better explanation of the Gentiles' occupation of the city?

The Gentile occupation of Jerusalem was interrupted at least once before, in 165 B.C., when Judas Maccabaeus successfully routed the army of Antiochus Epiphanes and rededicated the temple altar, which Antiochus had desecrated. Jewish rule over Jerusalem continued until the Roman general Pompey entered the city in 63 B.C. So a temporary occupation of Jerusalem by Israel need not mark the end of the times of the Gentiles. Such interruptions do not violate the meaning of the tense in Luke 21:24, where the verb gives the idea of a chronic condition which, of course, could include periods of change. The chronic condition of Jerusalem is Gentile domination, but there may be temporary relief of that condition.

One thing is certain. Whatever the immediate future of Jerusalem, a day is coming when the headlines will announce that Jerusalem is directly trodden down by the Gentiles. Even today, Gentile dominion is being exercised—but only indirectly. This will change during the Tribulation. The man of sin will first offer himself as the protector of Israel and Jerusalem. Then he will show his true colors and take over direct control of that city. He will turn on the people whom he vowed to defend. Only with the Second Coming of Christ will the man of sin be finally defeated and Jerusalem be made secure forever to the people of Israel. The times of the Gentiles will not end until that day arrives.

Then what significance is the present occupation of Jerusalem? It is important, because it has unified the city under a Jewish government and as the capital of Israel. The land, too, has been enlarged so that one nation now occupies most of Palestine. All of this will make it easier for the man of sin to make a covenant with the Jews, as he will do at the beginning of the Tribulation. It would seem that today the stage is set for the curtain to go up at any moment on the events of the Tribulation.

If that be so, the rapture of the church is imminent. We may be caught up any day to be with our Lord.

Same Theme Again

In reality, we have studied only one theme in this chapter—the times of the Gentiles. This is the period included in the image in Nebuchadnezzar's dream, beginning with the head (Nebuchadnezzar himself) and ending with the toes (Antichrist's 10-kingdom federation of Tribulation days). The same period was seen by Daniel in the vision recorded in chapter 7 of his book. Here, too, was the revelation of the little horn, the man of sin, the leader of the Federated States of Europe. His Gentile nations will again tread Jerusalem under foot in The Tribulation days, and his domination will be terminated only by the coming of Christ, who will bring victory over Antichrist, salvation for His people, and emancipation for Jerusalem, the holy city.

3
He Came as Promised

Being a prophet is a risky business.

The most obvious risk involves whether or not one's prophecies will come true. No prophet can stay in business long if he has too many failures, for he will soon be unmasked as a fraud. In spite of this, however, prophets have been plying their trade for thousands of years—with varying degrees of success.

The gift of prophecy is one of God's greatest gifts to the New Testament church, ranking second only to that of apostleship (1 Cor. 12:28). But from the beginning, there were false prophets. The Lord Jesus warned His followers against them (Matt. 7:15). Paul contested with one named Elymas on the island of Cyprus and struck him blind (Acts 13:6-11). John, near the end of New Testament times, declared that there were then *many* false prophets who had gone out into the world (1 John 4:1).

Apparently both true and false prophets continued to work in the churches, for interesting tests for prophets are found in a document written shortly before the close of the first century. This document is called the *Didaché*, or the "Teaching." It states that an itinerant prophet may be assumed to be false if he stays longer than three days in one house, or if he asks for money for himself, or if he does not practice what he preaches. It would seem that these are pretty good tests for *any* time!

In Old Testament times there were also tests for determining whether or not a person was a true prophet (Deut. 13:1-11; 18:20-22). He must speak in the name of the Lord. His prophecy should come to pass—a test which anyone (who lived long enough!) could easily apply to a prophet's words. If a so-called prophet failed either of these tests, he was to be stoned without mercy.

It was recognized that sometimes even false prophets might make accurate predictions. In such cases, another test was to be used. The substance of the prophet's message was to be measured against the commandments the Lord had previously given His people. If what the prophet taught differed from the body of truth already known, he was to be regarded as a false prophet even if the sign he had given came true. Like other false prophets, he was to be stoned. Obviously, it was risky business to practice prophecy.

Many Old Testament prophets not only prophesied but were willing to have their forecasts recorded so that they could easily be checked after the fulfillment had taken place. Of course, prophecies inspired by God came to pass exactly as predicted, and this fact is one of the best proofs for the authority of the Bible. It is also an indication that prophecies yet unfulfilled will come to pass exactly as made. Fulfilled prophecy is one of the greatest evidences of the divine origin of the Bible and its accuracy, inspiration, and authority.

We will study some of the prophecies that have *been* fulfilled— especially in relation to the first coming of Jesus Christ. We shall examine the exactness with which they came to pass and then, for comparison, try to determine the probability of their being fulfilled by chance. This should deepen our respect for the authority of the Bible in all the matters about which it speaks, and should confirm our faith in the trustworthiness of the prophecies which are yet to be fulfilled.

The Time of His Coming

One of the most amazing prophecies concerning the first coming of Christ is the prediction of the exact time of His coming. The prophecy is in Daniel 9:25: "Know therefore and understand, that from the going forth of the commandment to restore and to build Jerusalem unto the Messiah the Prince shall be seven weeks and threescore and two weeks. . . . " This is part of Daniel's great prophecy concerning the 70 sevens, and since we shall refer again to parts of this prophecy, we need to look at it in some detail.

Daniel had been concerned about Jeremiah's prophecy of the 70-year captivity (Jer. 25:11-12). Since Daniel knew that 70 years were almost over, he wondered what God would do next. So he fasted and prayed, and the answer came in the form of this prophecy concerning the 70 weeks, or "sevens"—a panoramic prediction of the entire history of the Jews. During 70 sevens, God said, all the things itemized in 25:24 would be accomplished.

The text does not say whether the "weeks" are periods of seven days or of seven years, but almost all scholars understand this prediction to mean 70 seven-year periods. There are two reasons for this: 70 weeks, less than a year and a half, simply is not enough time to bring in "everlasting righteousness." Further, when Daniel wants us to understand weeks of *days,* he uses the word "day" (10:2-3). The prediction, then, concerns 490 years. These years seem to be what are sometimes called "prophetic years"—that is, 360-day years—for the Scriptures use "1,260 days" as equivalent to "42 months," and both as equal to "time, times, and dividing of time" or three and a half years. These terms are equivalent only if they each are based on 360-day years, or prophetic years.

The 70 "sevens" began with "the commandment to restore and to build Jerusalem." Several dates are suggested for this event, but permission to build the city (not the temple) was given by Artaxerxes in 445 B.C. (Neh. 2:1-8). This, then, would be the date of the beginning of the 70 "weeks" of years. The 70 sevens are divided into three parts, as shown in figure 2.

After the first "week," or seven years, the city was rebuilt. After the second period, 434 years (or 483 years from the beginning), Messiah was to be cut off and Jerusalem destroyed (Dan. 9:26). Messiah was "cut off" (crucified) around A.D. 30, and Jerusalem was destroyed by the Romans under Titus in A.D. 70. So verse 26 tells us that the last, or 70th "week" does not follow *immediately* after the end of the 69th week. Actually, then, our diagram should look like figure 3.

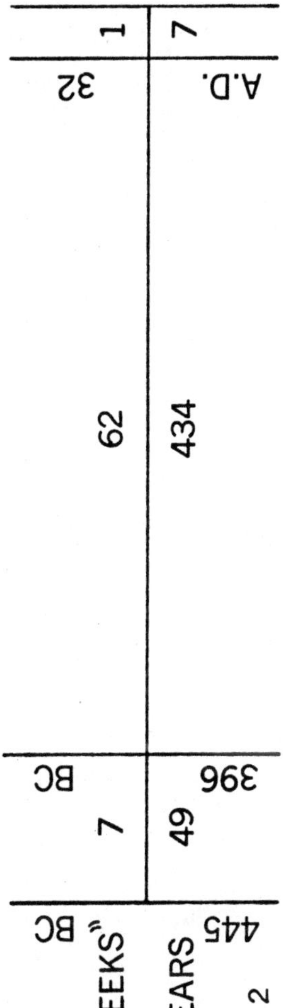

FIG. 2

"WEEKS" BC   7   62   1

YEARS   445 BC   49   396 BC   434   A.D.   32

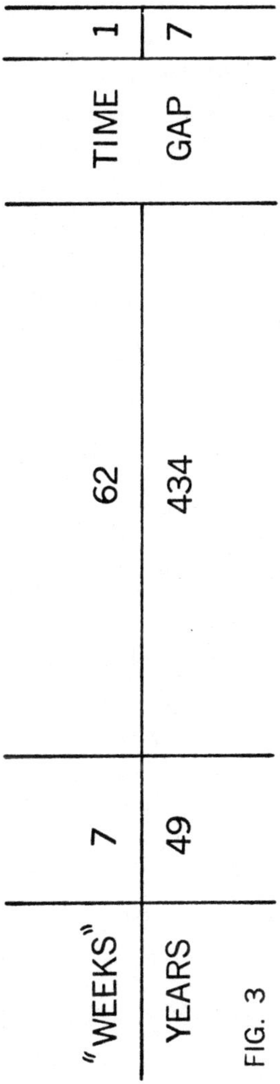

FIG. 3

"WEEKS"   7   62   TIME   1

YEARS   49   434   GAP   7

Again we are confronted by a time gap which the prophet did not anticipate. Between the end of the first 69 "weeks" of years and the final "week," there is a gap of unstated duration.

The prophecy of the 70 weeks concerns the time during which God deals with "thy [Daniel's] people and thy holy city"—i.e., with the Jews and with Jerusalem. Dispensationalists believe that since the Crucifixion, God has been dealing primarily with the Gentiles rather than with the Jews, but that He will resume His dealings with the Jews during the Tribulation period, just preceding the Millennium. They, therefore, mark the chart as shown in figure 4.

"WEEKS"	7	62	CHURCH	1	MILLENNIUM
YEARS	49	434	AGE	7	

FIG. 4

Our chief interest now is in the part of the prophecy that predicted the time of Messiah. After a total of 483 years Messiah would be alive, for it was at that time that He was to be cut off.

If the total number of prophetic years involved is multiplied by the number of prophetic days per year (483 × 360), we get 173,880 days. Starting with March 14, 445 B.C., the probable date of the commandment to rebuild Jerusalem, and adding 116 days for leap years, 173,880 days bring us to April 6, A.D. 32. This, according to Sir Robert Anderson, was the exact date of Palm Sunday the year Christ was crucified. Whether exactly to Palm Sunday or not, the computation does point to the end of Christ's life on earth, as predicted 5 centuries before by Daniel. Daniel is one prophet who need not be stoned!

To the Last Detail
"But thou, Bethlehem Ephratah, though thou be little among the thousands of Judah, yet out of thee shall He come forth unto Me that

is to be Ruler in Israel; whose goings forth have been from of old, from everlasting" (Micah 5:2).

Micah predicted Jesus' birthplace 700 years before Christ was born. The forecast must have seemed most unlikely at the time. Bethlehem was such a lowly place that it was never counted among Judah's possessions, but God was to exalt it by choosing it for the site of the Incarnation.

That Micah's prophecy was believed is evident from the ready answer the chief priests and scribes gave Herod when he inquired of them (Matt. 2:6). That the prophecy would be fulfilled would have seemed most unlikely, for Joseph and Mary lived in Nazareth, not Bethlehem. But a Roman tax decree brought them to Bethlehem during the last days of her pregnancy because Joseph was of the line of David and Bethlehem was David's city. That all these elements should combine at the right time would be highly improbable unless God were at work.

The manner of Messiah's birth was also predicted more than 700 years before He was born. "Behold, a virgin shall conceive, and bear a son, and shall call His name Immanuel" (Isa. 7:14). Some claim that this verse does not refer to the virgin birth, but the New Testament quotation of it (Matt. 1:23) uses a Greek word which admits no other meaning than "virgin." The prophecy had both a near and a far fulfillment. The near one assured Ahaz, to whom the sign was given, that the invasion of his kingdom would not be successful. The more remote fulfillment involved the virgin birth of Jesus. Since there has never been another baby born of only one human parent, this was a most unlikely prophecy for any time in history.

The Prophet Nathan predicted Messiah's lineage as being of the house of David (2 Sam. 7:12-13). Both Mary and Joseph were of that lineage, so that Jesus' claim to the throne of David has never been disputed on the ground of His family tree (Luke 1:31-33; Rom. 1:3). Long before the promise was even made to David, Jacob foretold that Messiah would come from the tribe of Judah (Gen. 49:10). Jesus fulfilled this prophecy, too (Heb. 7:14; Rev. 5:5).

Messiah was preceded by a forerunner, as Malachi had predicted 400 years before John the Baptist appeared in Palestine to fulfill prophecy (Mal. 3:1; Matt. 3:1-3).

So the 5 details concerning Messiah's birth—the place, the manner, the lineage, the tribe, and the forerunner—were prophesied from 400 to 1,600 years before He came. And He *came* as promised.

Biography in Advance

Christ's ministry was also predicted in the Old Testament. The chart below outlines some of the highlights. Forecast and fulfillment are perfectly matched, proving the accuracy of the Bible and the trustworthiness of God, who inspired it.

Christ's Ministry Predicted

Element of Christ's Ministry	Old Testament Prediction	New Testament Fulfillment
Location	Isa. 9:1-2	Matt. 4:13-16
Power	Isa. 11:2	Luke 3:22; 4:1
Saving Character	Isa. 61:1	Luke 4:16-19
Healing Character	Isa. 53:4	Matt. 8:16-17
Miracles	Isa. 35:5-6	Matt. 11:4-5
Inclusion of Gentiles	Isa. 42:1, 6	Luke 2:32
Zeal	Ps. 69:9	John 2:17
Serving Character	Isa. 42:1-4	Matt. 12:15-21
Humility	Zech. 9:9	Matt. 21:4-5
Rejection	Isa. 53:3	John 1:11

Forecasts of Jesus' Death

One of the most remarkable areas of fulfilled messianic prophecy concerns the events surrounding Jesus' death. These prophecies fall into two categories: (1) Old Testament predictions fulfilled precisely and fully by Christ's death; and (2) prophecies Christ Himself made, during His ministry, about His death. Old Testament prophecies include those listed on the chart "Christ's Death Predicted."

Christ's Death Predicted

Event of the Passion	Old Testament Prediction	New Testament Fulfillment
Deserted	Zech. 13:7	Matt. 26:31
Scourged and spat on	Isa. 50:6	Matt. 26:67
Given vinegar to drink	Ps. 69:21	Matt. 27:34, 48
Pierced with nails	Ps. 22:16	Luke 23:33
Forsaken by God	Ps. 22:1	Matt. 27:46
Surrounded by enemies	Isa. 22:7-8	Matt. 27:39-40
Numbered with transgressors	Isa. 53:12	Mark 15:28
Agonize with thirst	Ps. 22:15	John 19:28
Commend His spirit to God	Ps. 31:5	Luke 23:46
Have His garments distributed	Ps. 22:18	John 19:23-24
Have no bone broken	Ps. 34:20	John 19:33-36
Be buried with the rich	Isa. 53:9	Matt. 27:57-60
Rise from the dead	Ps. 16:9-10	Acts 2:27, 31
Ascend into glory	Ps. 68:18	Eph. 4:8

Christ's predictions about His death were definite and specific. At the Last Supper He said, "One of you shall betray Me" (Matt. 26:21), a prediction fulfilled by Judas that same night. Earlier, at Caesarea Philippi, the Lord had revealed that He would die in Jerusalem at the hands of the chief priests and scribes and be raised from the dead the third day (Matt. 16:21). He foretold the specific manner of His death as crucifixion (Matt. 20:19). In other words, He predicted the place, means, manner, and duration of His death—an extraordinary feat.

What is the special significance of these prophecies of our Lord concerning His death and resurrection? The angel who appeared to the two Marys at the tomb after Christ's resurrection answered that question: "Fear not ye, for I know that ye seek Jesus, which was crucified. He is not here, for He is risen as He said. Come, see the place where the Lord lay" (Matt. 28:5-6). The resurrection in Jerusalem on the third day was a validation of all Jesus had said.

The angel's emphasis seems to have been on "as He said." In other words, the angel reminded the women that all these events had been predicted by Christ. They should not have been surprised at what had happened, and now they should be more assured than ever of the truth of all His claims. The undisputable proof of His Messiahship was and is the empty tomb. A man who predicted His own resurrection and then rose as He promised is to be believed in all His claims.

We have examined only one kind of Old Testament prophecies—those dealing with the first coming of Christ. We have noted the exact fulfillments of predictions concerning His birth, ministry, death, and resurrection. These predictions were made by several prophets anywhere from 400 to 1,600 years before His birth.

In addition, we have noted some of the Lord's forecasts of His own death and resurrection, involving details which no man could possibly guess about his own death. But Christ was *not* guessing, as is proved particularly by His empty tomb. In fulfilling these prophecies, He validated all of the claims He had made during His ministry. He came, He ministered, He died, and He rose from the dead exactly as He and the prophets had promised.

The Odds Are Against It

Is it possible that the remarkable number and variety of prophecies concerning Christ's first coming could have been fulfilled by chance?

If you take a coin and flip it twice, the possibilities would be as follows: heads and heads, heads and tails, tails and heads, or tails and tails. The chance of heads turning up twice in a row is one out of four. Or, if four people each flipped a coin twice, one of them would come up with two heads in a row. This is the probability according to well-defined mathematical laws.

The chance of getting heads three times in a row without any other combination intervening is one out of eight. Or, if eight people were flipping coins, we could expect one of them to come up with three consecutive heads. Four heads in an uninterrupted sequence would require 16 people flipping.

If slightly more than 1,000 people were all flipping coins, the probability is that only one of them would turn up heads 10 times without any tails in the sequence. To achieve 20 heads in an unbroken succession would take more than a million people, and a run of 30 heads would take more than a billion. That is, if more than one fourth of the earth's total population were flipping coins, we could expect only one to come up with 30 heads in 30 tosses. A run of 40 would happen by chance less than once in a trillion times. Or, if all the people on 250 earths like ours were flipping coins, only one of them would come up with 40 uninterrupted heads in 40 tosses.

In this chapter we have noted 33 specific and detailed prophecies of the first coming of Christ, all of which were fulfilled exactly as predicted. Let us assume that each fulfilled prophecy is like a coin toss of "heads." According to the law of probability, if every person on the earth at the time our Lord came had been a prophet, we could not expect *one* of them to have predicted accurately all of these 33 things. Every living person would have had to be stoned as a false prophet, if they had depended on chance for the fulfillment of these prophecies.

There are, of course, many more than 33 prophecies concerning just the first advent of the Lord, so let's run the coin experiment further. Suppose we wanted a run of 100 heads without interruption, or 100 accurate prophecies. What would the probability be of accomplishing this by chance? This probability is one in as many times as is represented by a figure with more than 30 zeros.

Since a figure with 30 zeros is incomprehensible, we need a comparison that we can grasp. There are something like 200 billion stars in our Milky Way. Suppose each star were populated with four billion people—the number on earth. That would give you a figure with only 20 zeros—and we need 30. Suppose there were four billion people on each of the 200 billion stars of the Milky Way. According to mathematical probability, not one of them could by chance make 100 accurate predictions.

Someone has calculated that there are actually more than 300 prophecies concerning various aspects of the first coming of Christ. We can assuredly say that no one could possibly have made this number of accurate predictions *by chance*. But God did it, through His prophets, and the evidence is in the Bible for all to see and believe.

This is a startling proof of the divine origin of the Bible, and it concerns only one part of its prophecies—those connected with the first coming of Christ. There are many other equally specific prophecies in both the Old and the New Testaments which have also been fulfilled exactly as predicted. Add all these in with the ones we have referred to, and the *improbability* of their coming to pass increases at a fantastic rate to a point beyond any possible comprehension.

Authority and Assurance

The implications of the truths of this chapter lie in two principal areas—the area of *authority* and the area of *assurance*.

There is no finer objective proof of the authority of the Bible than fulfilled prophecy. By objective proof, we mean evidence that does *not* depend on personal experience. In other words, whether or not anyone ever has a personal experience of Christ's redemptive grace, he is still faced with the objective evidence of fulfilled prophecy.

How can it be explained? Chance is ruled out by the laws of probability. Only God could do something like this, and this makes the Bible, in which He has recorded the evidence, a uniquely authoritative Book. No other book, religious or secular, contains prophecies of the scope of the Bible's predictions, and no other book can begin to match the Bible's 100 percent record of fulfillment. Since the Bible's accurate prophecies prove that God inspired it, surely we can trust its history, doctrine, and other contents. We can study it with confidence, and heed its authority without reservation.

The same line of reasoning as we have applied to the Bible, the written Word, applies equally well to Christ, the living Word. The fulfilled predictions which He made are proof of *His* authority, too. Fulfilled prophecy validates His claims.

Fulfilled prophecy also gives us assurance concerning prophecies which are yet unfulfilled. We may, with all confidence, conclude from this study that since all the prophecies concerning Christ's first coming came to pass as predicted, then all the prophecies concerning His Second Coming will likewise be fulfilled exactly as they are written.

Because Jesus said, "I will come again" (John 14:3), we may be assured that He will. When Paul writes that the Lord shall descend from heaven, and that the dead in Christ will be raised and those alive in Christ will be changed (1 Thes. 4:16-17), we may confidently expect that just this will happen. When John predicts that the water of the Euphrates River will be dried up to facilitate the crossing of the armies of the kings of the east (Rev. 16:12), we can be certain that this will actually take place one day.

We may look ahead with complete confidence to the fulfilling of all of God's Word exactly as written. Our Lord said that not one jot or one tittle will remain unfulfilled (Matt. 5:17-18), which means that every letter, and each part of each letter of every word, will be fulfilled.

Yes, He came as God promised. And this means He will come *again* as He promised.

4
The
Jew and God's Promises

God chose the nation to be His son, His firstborn, His special people (Ex. 4:22; 19:5). And to Israel He gave specific promises that are the basis for many things that are yet to happen on this earth.

Whether the world understands it or not, the Jews are God's chosen people. This is stated and restated in God's Word. Abraham was called from his homeland to be the father of a great nation (Gen. 12:2). The Lord God acknowledged that nation as "My son, My firstborn" (Ex. 4:22). The choice was made from among all the nations: "For thou art an Holy people unto the Lord thy God, and the Lord hath chosen thee to be a peculiar people unto Himself, above all the nations that are upon the earth" (Deut. 14:2). The Jews were not chosen because of their merit but because God loved them. "The Lord did not set His love upon you, nor choose you, because ye were more in number than any people; for ye were the fewest of all people: But because the Lord loved you" (Deut. 7:7-8). This truth was reaffirmed even in the midst of defection and apostasy: "You only have I known of all the families of the earth" (Amos 3:2).

Even in New Testament times, when the church had entered the picture, God reaffirmed that His choice of Israel had not been set aside. "Hath God cast away His people?" Paul asked. And the reply is unmistakably clear: "God hath not cast away His people which He foreknew" (Rom. 11:1-2).

Promises to Abraham
God made a detailed covenant with Abraham, the father of the Chosen People (Gen. 12:1-3). The covenant was later confirmed and

amplified (Gen. 13:14-17; 15:1-7; 17:1-18). Personal promises were made to Abraham, national promises to Abraham's seed, and universal promises to all families of the earth.

The personal promises included God's special blessing upon Abraham in temporal things, for he acquired land, servants, cattle, silver, and gold (Gen. 13:14-15, 17; 15:7; 24:34-35). He was also blessed spiritually, and was a channel of blessing to others. He enjoyed communion with God and was called the friend of God (Gen. 18:17; James 2:23). All God's predictions about him came true.

Certain promises were also made to Abraham's descendants, the nation Israel. For one thing, God promised to continue the covenant with Abraham's children (Gen. 17:7). He promised that He would make them a great and innumerable nation (12:2; 13:16; 15:5). But most interesting, in the light of current events, was the promise to give Abraham's descendants, the Jews, a certain land for their own. The boundaries were specified (15:18), and the land was given as "an everlasting possession" (17:8).

Concerning all peoples, God promised that He would bless those who blessed Abraham and his descendants and curse those who cursed them. Throughout history, people *have* been blessed or cursed depending on their treatment of the Jews. This principle was established in Abraham's lifetime (14:12-20; 20:2-18) and during the experiences of the Children of Israel (Deut. 30:7; Isa. 14:1-2). In more recent times God has also dealt with nations on the basis of their treatment of the Jews. According to some interpreters, this will be the principle by which the Lord will judge Gentiles living at the conclusion of the Tribulation period—"Inasmuch as ye have done it unto one of the least of these My brethren [the Jews], ye have done it unto Me" (Matt. 25:40).

This principle raises the interesting question about the role of the United States in future events. Some Bible teachers think the U.S. will be part of the revived Roman Empire, the ten-nation federation headed by Antichrist in the Tribulation. This may be the case, for certainly historic and ethnic ties link the U.S. to western Europe. But if this is true, the role apparently will not be an important one, for the U.S. is not named, mentioned, or hinted at either directly or symbolically in any of the prophecies concerning the Western Federation of nations of the Tribulation.

Some think the United States will be preserved as a nation, even though it will not be dominant in world affairs in the Tribulation, simply because this country has not overtly persecuted the Jews. They say that because of this, God will keep His promise, made so long ago to Abraham, and not bring judgment on America—though she otherwise deserves it.

There is some support for this line of reasoning, for certainly the Jewish people have fared well in America. They have taken their place in all phases of life. Anti-Semitism here is not strong. The United States was one of the first countries to recognize the State of Israel after its creation in 1948. Much of the money to sustain Israel has come from the American government and from American Jews who have done well in the U.S.

The second universal promise of the Abrahamic covenant is this: "In thee [Abraham] shall all the families of the earth be blessed" (Gen. 12:3). This promise is to be understood as broadly as it is stated. Abraham himself was such a great blessing to all nations, that he is revered by Jews, Muslims, and Christians. Israel has blessed the world by being the channel through which God sent His revelation in the Bible (Rom. 3:2). Christ, as *the* Seed of Abraham (Gal. 3:16), has by His coming blessed the entire world.

Promised Real Estate

One of the promises constantly reiterated in the covenant with Abraham concerned Palestine. Abraham was told, in the original promise, to leave Ur, his own country, for "a land that I will show thee." Furthermore, the land was promised to his people forever, and most interestingly, the boundaries were specifically outlined as being "from the river of Egypt unto the great river, the river Euphrates" (Gen. 15:18).

Concerning the eastern boundary, the river Euphrates, there is no question, but what is meant by "the river of Egypt" has been debated. The question is whether this is a reference to the Nile or to a stream called the Wadi-el-Arish, not far from Gaza. Actually two different Hebrew words are used for river and wadi and the word used in Genesis 15:18 for both the Euphrates and the river of Egypt is *not* the one which means wadi. A wadi is a stream that is full only after the rains and dry the rest of the year, while the word for river indicates a stream that flows all the year round. This distinction is made in Isaiah 27:12, where the wadi is called "stream" in our English translation. But the word used in Genesis 15:18 is the word for river and it seems that it can only refer to the Nile. On a map the two "rivers" are located as shown in figure 5.

One of the interesting results of the Six-Day War in June 1967 was that the armies of Israel pushed past the Wadi-el-Arish toward the Nile, though they stopped at the Suez Canal. However, under the terms of the March 1979 peace treaty with Egypt, Israel has already returned two thirds of the Sinai to Egypt, including the town of El Arish, and is scheduled to return the remainder before April 1982.

Since the eastern boundary is the Euphrates, Israel must occupy a great deal of territory before God's promise will have been fulfilled. It is possible Israel may not regain this territory till the Millennium, when Christ reigns on earth; but undoubtedly she will continue to make efforts to get it.

In all her history, Israel has never occupied all the land given in God's original promise. Even under the extensive and glorious reign of Solomon, much of the land was only under tribute, and its boundaries extended only to the border of Egypt (1 Kings 4:21). Someday, though, the promise will be fulfilled.

To be sure, some contingencies are involved in the intermediate fulfillments of this promise. Throughout Israel's history, obedience was God's condition for possessing the land, and dispersion was the result of disobedience (Deut. 28:30; Jer. 25:11). When Israel realizes

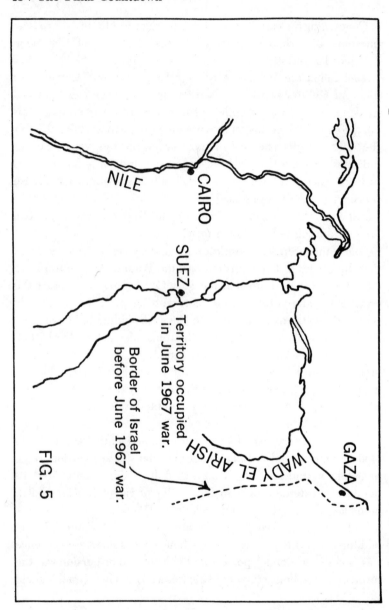

FIG. 5

the ultimate fulfillment of the promise, she will be obedient under the rule of Christ.

Must We or Will He?

Whether or not the Abrahamic promises were conditional or unconditional is an important question. If they were conditioned by the Jew's faithfulness or goodness, we can assume the Jews have forfeited any claims to Palestine and the other blessings included in the covenant, for they have sinned repeatedly. If, on the other hand, the promises were conditioned only on God's faithfulness, they will be fulfilled in spite of man's failure.

The answer to this question is found in what God did to confirm the covenant recorded in Gensis 15:9-17. Particularly emphasized were the promises concerning the continuation of Abraham's seed and the possession of the land. God solemnized the covenant by sacrificing animals and laying the severed parts on the ground. Ordinarily, the two parties to the agreement would walk together between the parts of the sacrifice, but on this occasion instead of both God and Abraham walking between the pieces of the sacrifice, God put Abraham to sleep and passed alone between the parts of the animals. God could not have shown more clearly that the keeping of this covenant was reaffirmed to Abraham's son, Isaac, and to *his* son Jacob, (Gen. 26:2-4; 28:13-15). No conditions were attached in either instance, and the reaffirmation was made on the basis of the oath with which God made the covenant with Abraham. Abraham sinned during the years between the making of the covenant and its confirmation to Isaac, so if God viewed the covenant as conditioned on obedience, He would have had ample reason for abrogating His promise. Instead He reaffirmed it. This is further evidence that the covenant was unconditional as far as involving any human responsibility.

Promises to David

God also made important promises to David. The record of what is usually called the Davidic Covenant is in 2 Samuel 7:12-16. God promised that Solomon, not David, would build the temple, and that David's lineage, throne, and kingdom would be established forever. All conservatives agree that Christ is the Seed of David who is the ultimate Fulfiller of the promise. This link was supplied by the angel at the announcement of Christ's birth: "And the Lord God shall give unto Him the throne of His father David: and He shall reign over the house of Jacob forever; and of His kingdom there shall be no end" (Luke 1:32-33).

These promises concerning the King and the kingdom were often repeated in the Old Testament. The most forceful statement of them is in Psalm 89, where the Lord warned of chastisement for disobedience but said that the covenant would not be broken or altered in any way (vv. 30-37). Isaiah prophesied that Messiah would sit on the throne of His father David and that His kingdom would be established forever (Isa. 9:6-7), other prophets predicted additional features of this Davidic-Messianic kingdom (Jer. 23:5-6; 30:8-9; 33:4-21; Ezek. 37:24-25; Dan. 7:13-14; Hosea 3:4-5; Amos 9:11; Zech. 14:4-9).

All agree that the Lord Jesus Christ is the One who fulfills the promises concerning the Seed and the Davidic throne and kingdom, but the question is, *When?* Is He now sitting in heaven on the throne of His father David, and is the Davidic kingdom the present heavenly rule of Christ over His church? Or, will the Davidic kingdom be on earth in the Millennium, when Christ will rule here? The view one chooses affects his entire picture of the future.

Post-, A-, or Pre- and the Millennium

You have probably heard the terms postmillennial, amillennial, and premillennial, but note the relationship between them and the promises God made to Abraham and to David.

"Millennium" means a thousand years, and it refers to the time of the kingdom promised to David. In other words, millennialism has to do with one's view of the kingdom.

Postmillennialism is so labeled because it teaches that the Second

Coming of Christ will occur *after* (post) the Millennium. Postmillen-arians look for a utopian state on earth to be brought about through the noble efforts of the church. During this "golden age," the church, not Israel will receive the fulfillment of the promises to Abraham and David. The kingdom will be on earth, but it will be a church kingdom, not a Jewish one, and the King, Christ, will be absent from the earth, not present on it; He will rule in the hearts of His people. The Lord Himself will return afterward. The basic postmillennial scheme looks like this:

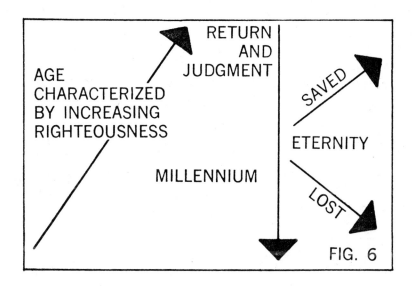

AGE CHARACTERIZED BY INCREASING RIGHTEOUSNESS

RETURN AND JUDGMENT

SAVED

ETERNITY

MILLENNIUM

LOST

FIG. 6

Amillennialism denies that there will be any kind of earthly millennial kingdom in the future. The kingdom is *now;* it is heaven's rule over the church. The amillenarian feels that the promise concerning the possession of Palestine by Abraham's descendants need not be fulfilled because the Jewish people broke the covenant by their disobedience to God. The only millennium we can expect, according to this viewpoint, is the rule of Christ now in heaven, where He is seated on the throne of David. The basic amillennial scheme looks like this:

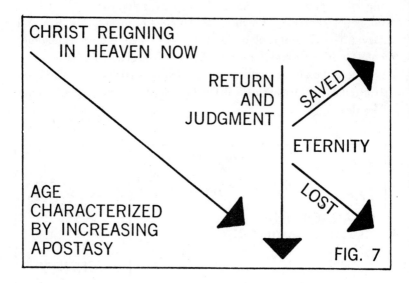

CHRIST REIGNING IN HEAVEN NOW

RETURN AND JUDGMENT

SAVED

ETERNITY

AGE CHARACTERIZED BY INCREASING APOSTASY

LOST

FIG. 7

Premillennialism holds that the Second Coming of Christ will precede the millennial kingdom, and that Christ, not the church (as in postmillennialism) will be the One to bring in the kingdom. Christ will actually reign on earth as King, and during that time the Jewish people will experience the full blessing of the promises made to Abraham and David. Among premillenarians there are different views as to when the rapture of the church will occur in relation to the Tribulation. These will be discussed in chapter 7. The basic outline of the premillennial viewpoint is shown in figure 8.

I am a premillennialist because I think it unwise to take the words of the Bible in a nonliteral sense when the literal meaning is plain. These promises to Abraham and David concern the physical descendants of Abraham. Why expect them to be fulfilled by the church, unless Israel no longer means *Israel* but means the *church*?

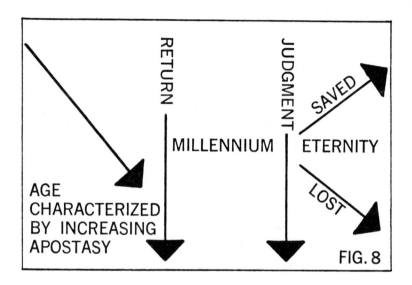

RETURN

JUDGMENT

SAVED

MILLENNIUM | ETERNITY

LOST

AGE
CHARACTERIZED
BY INCREASING
APOSTASY

FIG. 8

Since the New Testament continues to distinguish the Jews from the church, it appears that we should expect these promises to be fulfilled through the Jews rather than the church (1 Cor. 10:32; Rom. 11:26).

The other viewpoints don't provide for a time in which the promises (especially the one that guarantees possession of Palestine) can be fulfilled by the people to whom they were promised. The postmillenarians' Golden Age is for the church, and amillennialism has no period at all after the conclusion of the Church Age. Only premillennialism includes a time during which these promises to Israel (seed, land, throne, kingdom) can be fulfilled.

Therefore, premillenarians expect the headlines to announce, one day, that Christ has come to rule and to set up His kingdom on earth, the Jewish people are dwelling safely in the Promised Land, and that the throne of David, occupied by the Son of David, has been established in Jerusalem. That will be the complete fulfillment of God's promises.

Persecution and Preservation

One of the most improbable facts of world history has been the survival of the Jewish nation. But God said this would be so (Jer. 31:35-36). Discipline in the form of dispersion has come to the Jews, but their continuance as a people has never been in jeopardy, nor will it be.

About 300 years after David was promised that his house and kingdom would be established forever, the 10 northern tribes of Israel were taken into captivity in Samaria. A little more than a century later the two southern tribes were carried into Babylon, making the dispersion complete. There the Jews remained, though always racially distinct, until the edict of Cyrus in 538 B.C. allowed some of them to return to rebuild Jerusalem and the temple.

During the 400 years between the close of the Old Testament and the birth of Christ, tens of thousands of Jews were slaughtered and sold into slavery. On one occasion, Antiochus Epiphanes (175-164 B.C.) killed 40,000 Jews and sold an equal number into bondage simply because they had begun to celebrate his supposed death. When Rome conquered Palestine before the birth of Christ, more Jews were killed or sold into slavery.

In A.D. 70, the Jews suffered an even greater calamity. Two years before Gentiles killed 20,000 Jews in Caesarea and, in a single day, the people of Damascus cut the throats of 10,000 more. But in A.D. 70, troops conquered the Jerusalem temple. Soldiers hurled more than 100,000 bodies of Jews over the city wall during that seige, and after the fall of the city an equal number were sold into slavery. One estimate is that more than a million people were killed in the conquest of Jerusalem and the events that followed.

The world has not been any kinder to the Jewish people since that time. Under Emperor Hadrian (A.D. 117-138), the Romans destroyed 985 towns in Palestine and killed 580,000 men. Many others were sold into slavery. The Jews were banished from Jerusalem, a policy continued under other emperors. The Crusades (A.D. 1096 and following), which sought to recapture the holy places in Palestine from the Muslims, also brought extermination to the Jews of Europe as part of the holy wars. Even the English and the French, as late as the 13th century, wiped out entire Jewish communities in their countries. While Columbus was discovering America, the Jews were being expelled from almost all of western Europe.

Yet all of these persecutions appear tame in comparison with what happened to the Jews under Hitler during World War II. It is estimated that more than six million Jews were exterminated, and this in the 20th century, a supposedly civilized era.

The persecution and preservation of the Jews throughout history has been a fulfillment of prophecy. Through Moses, the Lord predicted the Jews' dispersion "from one end of the earth even unto the other" (Deut. 28:64) and their persecution: "Thy life shall hang in doubt before thee" (Deut. 28:66). Our Lord, confirming the promise made to David of the perpetuity of his seed, guaranteed that the nation (a more exact rendering of "generation" in Matt. 24:34) will continue to exist as an entity right through the entire Tribulation period. Persecution, dispersion, slaughter, slavery, and intermarriage would have eradicated the Jews except that God has promised they will continue as a people to fulfill His predicted purposes. Nothing else could account for their unique history.

But what of the unfulfilled promises in those covenants to Abraham and David? Will the Jews *really* possess the *entire* land of Palestine? Will Messiah's kingdom *actually* be established on earth? Certainly all of God's past dealings with the Jews encourage us to believe that these promises will also come to pass.

5
Israel and Her Future

New nations have been born with such frequency in the past several decades that we have come to accept them as commonplace. We are used to having a war going on somewhere in the world. But the birth of one certain nation and its "little" wars are of great prophetic significance.

That nation, Israel, declared her independence May 15, 1948. The Six-Day War that began June 5, 1967 was the conflict. Why should a little nation in a little war attract so much attention? What do these events mean in relation to Bible prophecy?

They Will Return

Though the slaughter of Jews during World War II was devastating, the promises of Israel's return are still in God's Word. They are specific, too: "And it shall come to pass in that day, that the Lord shall set His hand again the second time to recover the remnant of His people, which shall be left, from Assyria, and from Egypt, and from Pathros, and from Cush, and from Elam, and from Shinar, and from Hamath, and from the islands of the sea. And He shall set up an ensign for the nations, and shall assemble the outcasts of Israel, and gather together the dispersed of Judah from the four corners of the earth" (Isa. 11:11-12).

Notice particularly the phrase "the second time." The first captivity was known as the Babylonian captivity, and it lasted 70 years. From it, some Jews returned to Palestine to restore Jerusalem and rebuild the temple. But under the Roman rule, the Jews were dispersed (A.D. 70) to all corners of the earth. The return from this dispersion is "the second time" Isaiah spoke of. This return will bring Jews from all parts of the world—not simply from Babylon, as the first time.

Furthermore, the prediction of this return includes repossession of Palestine: "But the Lord liveth, that brought up the Children of Israel from the land of the north, and from all the lands whither He had driven them: and I will bring them again into their land that I gave unto their fathers" (Jer. 16:15). "They shall inherit the land forever" (Isa. 60:21). "For I will take you from among the heathen, and gather you out of all countries, and will bring you into your own land" (Ezek. 36:24).

This return will be the final one, for the prophets also predicted that when the people return on this occasion there will be no further dispersion of them: "And I will bring again the captivity of My people of Israel, and . . . I will plant them upon their land, and they shall no more be pulled up out of their land which I have given them, saith the Lord thy God" (Amos 9:14-15).

It is important to notice, particularly in light of the spiritual condition of most Jews today, that their final return will be accompanied by spiritual cleansing and regeneration. This promise is carefully interwoven with the promises of the return. "A new heart also will I give you, and a new spirit will I put within you: and I will take away the stony heart out of your flesh, and I will give you a heart of flesh. And I will put My Spirit within you, and cause you to walk in My statutes, and ye shall keep My judgments, and do them. And ye shall dwell in the land that I gave to your fathers; and ye shall be My people, and I will be your God" (Ezek. 36:26-28).

The vision of the valley of dry bones, which follows this promise, pictures the new life Israel will experience when she returns to the land. The vision of the two sticks (37:15-28) pictures the unity of the people which God will bring about when He regathers them. The promise of cleansing is reiterated in this vision: "Neither shall they defile themselves any more with their idols, nor with their detestable things, nor with any of their transgressions: but I will . . . cleanse them: so shall they be My people, and I will be their God" (v. 23). Of course, Israel has not yet been cleansed of sin (except for those individual Jews who accept Christ as Saviour), so whatever is happening in Israel today cannot be the *complete* fulfillment of these prophecies.

To review: the prophesied return of the Jews to Palestine will (1) be from all the earth, not merely from Babylon; (2) bring them to Palestine; (3) not be followed by any further dispersion; (4) include prosperity in the land; (5) be accompanied by a *spiritual* rebirth for the nation. All this is plain and certain.

How Zionism Began

Until this present century there had been no movement of the Jews back to Palestine in all the Christian era. Indeed, even as late as the 19th century, their loss of Palestine was accepted by many Jews, and the idea of their ever returning was kept alive more by premillennial Christians than by anyone else. However, toward the end of the 19th century, persecution of the Jews in Russia and anti-Semitism in Germany forced many Jews to think of the possibility of setting up a colony of Jewish people in Palestine.

The first Zionist Congress was held in Basle, Switzerland in 1897, under the direction of Theodor Herzl. Its stated goal was "to create for the Jewish people a home in Palestine secured by public law." This was more of a political than a religious movement. Its aim was the granting of some sort of charter as a prerequisite for colonization of Palestine. This charter came in the form of the famous Balfour Declaration, issued on November 2, 1917; it said in part: "His Majesty's Government view with favour the establishment in Palestine of a national home for the Jewish people, and will use their best endeavours to facilitate the achievement of this object, it being clearly understood that nothing shall be done which may prejudice the civil and religious rights of existing non-Jewish communities in Palestine, or the rights and political status enjoyed by Jews in any other country." In the same year, British General Allenby captured

Jerusalem, which led some to think that perhaps they were seeing the beginning of the fulfillment of Old Testament prophecy.

The Balfour Declaration gave impetus to the settling of Palestine. Chaim Weizmann, who had succeeded Herzl as leader of the World Zionist Movement, declared: "Wherever we look upon the Jewish map of the world, we find that all roads lead to Palestine. There have arisen some mirages in the desert, but these have served only to confuse the issue and still further disillusion the Jewish people. Contemporary history has impressed upon us the fact (which many of us have long been unwilling to acknowledge) that the salvation of Jewry and the rescue of individual Jews are alike inextricably bound up with the accelerated upbuilding of the Jewish National Home in Palestine."

The Balfour Declaration gave Zionism the political charter and long-awaited guarantee which opened the door for an enlarged Zionist program. The Jewish population in Palestine has grown rapidly, with an ever-increasing proportion of the total population being Jews rather than Arabs.

In 1882, there were approximately 24,000 Jews in Palestine, out of a total population of 624,000. In 1890, there were 47,000. In 1914, there were 85,000 Jews in a total population of 700,000. In 1927, there were 150,000; in 1931, 175,000; in 1936, 404,000; in 1941, 505,000 out of a total population of 1.6 million; in 1945, 600,000; in 1948, when the new nation was born, there were about 650,000 Jews in Palestine. In 1978 the population was estimated to be 3,689,000.

Of course, this influx of Jews did not please the resident Arab populace, and the mounting tensions and strife caused Great Britain to turn over the problem to the United Nations. On November 29, 1947 the U.N. proposed a partition of Palestine into a Jewish and an Arab state, with the city of Jerusalem an international city under U.N. control. The plan was rejected by the Arabs; six months of confusion followed, including speeded-up immigration of Jews into Palestine. The British terminated their mandate over Palestine and the next day (May 15, 1948) the new state of Israel was declared in existence. The war that followed between Jews and Arabs ended in an uneasy truce. The armistice drawn in 1949 lasted for the next 18 years, until the Six-Day War in 1967.

That armistice carved out about 8,000 square miles of territory for the State of Israel. After the Jewish victory in 1967, the area was more than quadrupled, with the addition of conquered territory in Syria, Samaria, and Sinai. But perhaps the most important part of the Six-Day-War victory was the capture of Jerusalem. Up to that time there were two Jerusalems—the new city on the west, which had become the capital of Israel, and the old walled city and its suburbs on the east, which belonged to Jordan. Separated by no-man's-land for 19 years, the two parts of the city were united by the Israeli victory. This gave the Jewish people access to their most sacred site, the Wailing Wall, and generated a lot of talk about the possible building of a new temple in Jerusalem.

Over the protests of many nations, a resolution of the United Nations, and a plea from Pope Paul, the uniting of Jerusalem has been cemented in every way possible. Public utilities have been integrated, streets have been joined, and the no-man's-land has been completely erased. The swiftness with which events have moved was displayed in a headline in *The Jerusalem Post* on May 6, 1968, less than a year after the Six-Day War. It proudly said, "600,000 See 20th Birthday Fete in United Jerusalem." Who would have thought this even remotely possible just a few years ago?

Jerusalem's Future

More and more, Jerusalem will appear in the headlines. Israel is at the confluence of three continents, and Jerusalem is her capital. Militarily and economically, this is a strategic part of the world, and Jerusalem is at the hub of it all.

The immediate future for Jerusalem, to the end of this age and the rapture of the church, will not be a secure one. Israel will do everything in her power to hold Jerusalem as part of her territory. As her leaders have often said, "Jerusalem is not negotiable." This does not mean, however, that the city could not be taken from Israel by force. It may be that, in another round of war, Jerusalem will change hands again. In fact, this could happen several times before the Rapture. But after the Rapture, when the Tribulation begins, Jerusalem will evidently be in Israeli hands, since Antichrist's covenant with Israel involves the temple in Jerusalem. Apparently Israel will feel threatened; otherwise, why would she enter into a covenant with the stronger western powers?

Jerusalem's road will not be an easy one, even with the backing of the man of sin and the nations of his federation. Concerning Jerusalem's future to the end of the Tribulation, Daniel predicted war and desolations (Dan. 9:26). In chapter 8 we shall study the various alliances of nations and their movements in and out of Palestine. Jerusalem will be in the midst of much confusion and will not know permanent peace until she receives the Prince of Peace.

The campaign of Armageddon (the word "battle," in Revelation 16:14, means a series of battles, or campaign) will also involve Jerusalem, at the end of the Tribulation. Zechariah prewrote the news story, which does not paint a very pretty picture: "For I will gather all nations against Jerusalem to battle; and the city shall be taken, and the houses rifled, and the women ravished; and half of the city shall go forth into captivity, and the residue of the people shall not be cut off from the city (Zech. 14:2). When the Lord returns in the midst of this campaign there will be upheavals that will change the topography of the land around Jerusalem (Zech. 14:4-5, 8, 10-11). Then the city will begin the period of her greatest glory—the millennial age.

But we must back up to the first part of the Tribulation to note another event. It will take place in Jerusalem and will be headlined throughout the world. It is the building of another temple in Jerusalem. There must be a temple there during the Tribulation, for the man of sin, as part of his treaty with Israel, will guarantee the rights of the people to practice their ancient temple worship once again. What is more, when Antichrist, in the middle of the

Tribulation, breaks his covenant, he himself will sit in the temple demanding worship as God (Dan. 9:27; 2 Thes. 2:4; Matt. 24:15).

No sooner had the guns cooled from the Six-Day War in 1967, than speculation arose over the possibility of rebuilding the temple. Even *Time* magazine devoted almost a page to the matter. One major obstacle, at the moment, is that Islam's sacred mosque, the Dome of the Rock, stands on the site of the former temples—the site where Israel would undoubtedly wish to build again. But, as one Israeli said about this problem, "Who knows? Perhaps there will be an earthquake." There *will* be a temple, for the Bible says so. It will be in Jerusalem. The Bible does not specifically say *where* in Jerusalem, though it is difficult to see how the Jews would be satisfied with anything less than the former site. The temple will be in use during the Tribulation. Construction *may* begin even before the rapture of the church, but that is not necessary, for a temple could be erected in a matter of weeks once the people had the go-ahead.

Other things that will occur in Jerusalem during the Tribulation include the slaying of the two witnesses (Rev. 11:8), the reign of the man of sin (Matt. 24:15), an earthquake that will destroy one-tenth of the city and 7,000 inhabitants (Rev. 11:13), and battles in connection with the war to be fought at the close of the period.

Then Christ will come. He shall stand on the Mount of Olives east of Jerusalem, and then, *only then*, will that great city experience the meaning of her name—City of Peace. The glory of the city, during the Millennium that follows, will be unexcelled. It will be the center of government, "for out of Zion shall go forth the Law, and the Word of the Lord from Jerusalem" (Isa. 2:3). It will be a happy place: "Thus saith the Lord; I am returned unto Zion, and will dwell in the midst of Jerusalem: and Jerusalem shall be called a city of truth; and the mountain of the Lord of hosts the holy mountain. Thus saith the Lord of hosts, There shall yet old men and old women dwell in the streets of Jerusalem, and every man with his staff in his hand for every age. And the streets of the city shall be full of boys and girls playing in the streets thereof" (Zech. 8:3-5). Many other passages predict Jerusalem's exalted position and glory (Isa. 52:1-12; 66:10-14; Jer. 3:17). The city which will be the focal point of war during the Tribulation will become the center of the government and worship of the Prince of Peace in the Millennium.

Where Will Israel Go?

Where does the nation Israel go from here? The prophecies concerning Israel's regathering to the Land of Palestine which we have surveyed have not been fulfilled by the existence of the State of Israel. For one thing, not all Jews are in Israel; for another, they are not redeemed, as they will be in the final regathering; for yet another, the full and final return will be expedited by angels (Matt. 24:31), not airplanes.

Nevertheless, the existence of the present political entity that we call Israel is extremely significant in the light of prophecy. A Jewish nation must be functioning in order to make a treaty with the man of sin at the beginning of the Tribulation. Israel as it exists today could very well be that nation. Between now and that time, her fortunes could rise and fall several times, but when the Tribulation begins, Israel will be a nation and will be looking for assistance from the European federation of nations.

During the first part of the Tribulation, Israel's fortunes will rise; during the last part, they will plummet. All will go well for three-and-a-half years under the protection of the man of sin. The practice of Judaism in the temple will be restored. The military security of the nation will seem inviolable. Undoubtedly the mineral wealth of the Dead Sea will insure prosperity. But Israel's fortunes will drastically and suddenly change at the midpoint of the seven years of Tribulation, when Antichrist breaks his covenant with the Jewish people and makes them objects of fearful persecution.

The Lord warned of this time in no uncertain terms. He said that when the Jews then living see the man of sin standing in the temple demanding worship, they should flee from Judea to any refuge they can find. He warned them to leave without any delay, not even to linger long enough to pack clothes. He suggested that they pray that this will not happen either in winter (when the weather will hinder travel) or on the Sabbath (when lack of public transportation will slow down their escape).

That the Jews will be the particular object of persecution is clear from the prophecy (Rev. 12:13-17). In this passage, the woman represents Israel, the one who bore Christ (v. 5). The dragon is clearly Satan (v. 9), and he makes Israel the special focus of his persecution (v. 13). As the Jews are fleeing Judea, God will evidently step in and help His people by sustaining them in a place in the wilderness for the three and a half years of this intense persecution (v. 13). But Satan will not let them alone; he will attack them with a flood in their place of refuge, apparently to try to drown them out of their hiding place. But God will intervene again by making the earth open (possibly in an earthquake) to consume the water of the flood and save those persecuted people from drowning.

When Satan realizes that he cannot kill the group that has fled into the wilderness, he will turn his wrath (through the Antichrist and the false prophet) to the rest of the Jews, who did not flee (v. 17). So terrible will be this time of persecution that the Lord said no one would survive except for the fact that the days will be shortened. If it were allowed to continue, the persecution would destroy everyone; only the coming of Christ will bring this awful time to an end.

Israel will be saved at the Second Coming of Christ: "And so all Israel shall be saved: as it is written, There shall come out of Zion the Deliverer, and shall turn away ungodliness from Jacob, for this is My covenant unto them, when I shall take away their sins" (Rom. 11:26-27). At this time Jews who have survived the Tribulation days will be judged (we shall study the details in chapter 10). Those who successfully survive this judgment (all rebels will be purged) will be saved and will enter the millennial kingdom. This will fulfill all the promises concerning Israel's complete regathering and salvation.

During the Millennium, Israel's position will be glorious. She will be exalted above the Gentiles. "And strangers [Gentiles] shall stand

and feed your flocks, and the sons of the alien shall be your plowmen and your vine-dressers. But ye shall be named the priests of the Lord; men shall call you the ministers of our God: ye shall eat the riches of the Gentiles, and in their glory shall ye boast yourselves" (Isa. 61:5-6).

Israel will again be related to God "by marriage." "And I will betroth thee unto Me forever; yea, I will betroth thee unto Me in righteousness, and in judgment, and in lovingkindness, and in mercies" (Hosea 2:19). Israel will be the means of bringing praise to God: "At that time will I bring you again, even in the time that I gather you, for I will make you a name and a praise among all people of the earth, when I turn back your captivity before your eyes, saith the Lord" (Zeph. 3:20).

Finally, in that time Israel will worship the Lord in the most favorable of all climates. Satan will be bound; Christ will be reigning; the Holy Spirit will be working in special ways (Isa. 32:15; Ezek. 36:27), and apparently the people will participate in the glories of the temple worship, a memorial to the sacrifice of Christ. A deep and satisfying spiritual life will be the portion of the nation in that day.

Word of Warning

What you have studied so far is probably making you think that the coming of the Lord cannot be far away. A western European federation of nations could be formed almost overnight. Israel's birth and rise to a place of importance is one of the most astounding facts of modern history. The increasing attention focused on Jerusalem, and the talk of a new temple, are matters we would not have dreamed of a few years ago. There *is* a Jewish political state in Palestine, and Jewish people *are* returning to that land every day. These are realities of our times.

All this is significant. Our Lord said, "When ye shall see all these things, know that it is near, even at the doors" (Matt. 24:33), and certainly today we are seeing many signs happening *at the same time*, a condition which has not been true in any previous time. A true

Christian cannot help but rejoice in the knowledge that all this seems to indicate that at any day the church may be caught up to be with the Lord forever. This prospect delights the heart of a child of God.

But let's think a step further. The Jews are going back to Palestine and their nation has been established there. But they are going back *in unbelief*. Today's chosen people are just as much under the condemnation of sin as anybody else. True, the future for Israel is a glorious one, but before the glory there will be intense suffering and persecution, which will take the lives of many. If the Lord should come for His church within the next few years, many unsaved Jews who have gone back to Palestine will be killed by Antichrist and in the judgments of the wrath of God, and will spend eternity in the lake of fire.

That the Jews are chosen people, or that they are being used in the working out of the prophetic purposes of God, does not in any way mean that they can be saved, today, apart from personal faith in Jesus Christ. A Christian can rejoice at what he sees taking place in Palestine, but he should also be sad when he reflects on the lost spiritual condition of the people to whom it is happening.

The same paradoxical feelings come to a believer when he thinks of the coming of Christ. This prospect brings joy to his heart, but it also reminds him that after Christians have been taken up there will be no further opportunities to do for God the things we always planned to get around to "someday."

What I am telling you is what the Lord told John in the vivid drama recorded in Revelation 10:8-11. The book which John was commanded to eat was pleasant to taste but bitter to digest. Prophetic truth is pleasant to the taste, but the contemplation of its full implications may bring heaviness of heart. We rejoice in the revelation of coming triumph and glory; we are distressed at the present lost condition of multitudes and the knowledge that terrible judgments will precede coming glory.

6
What's
Ahead for the Church?

"The church will not fail," assured the announcer in soothing tones suitable to his radio program, "Inspiration Time." But a reassuring voice is no guarantee that a speaker is telling the truth.

What is the future for the church? *Will* it succeed—or fail? How does the ecumenical movement fit into the prophetic picture? Such questions are answered in the prophetic portions of the Bible—and, of course, these answers are true.

The Church and the Churches

The radio announcer's statement needs clarification because we are not exactly sure what he meant by "church." The word has various meanings, both in current usage and in the Bible. We must understand these different meanings before we can discuss the future for the church.

The word for church, as it appears in the New Testament, means an assembly. The kind of people involved and the purpose for which they assemble are not really expressed by the word itself. For instance, the "town meeting" type of gathering which the city of Ephesus held under certain circumstances was called a "church," or assembly (Acts 19:39, 41)—the very same word.

Usually, however, the New Testament word is used for what is more commonly understood as the *church*, but even this idea has several meanings. For instance, the church is spoken of as the body of Christ (Eph. 1:22-23; Col. 1:18). This includes all true believers in Christ, who are said to be joined to Christ, the Head of the body (1 Cor. 12:12-13). Many members of the body of Christ have already died and are with the Lord in His presence, but some are still alive. Some of them are living holy lives; other are carnal Christians. Most are members of local churches; some may not be. They are scattered throughout the whole earth, but all of them have been born again.

The question, Will *this* church fail? is specific and can be given a clear-cut answer—NO! And the future for *this* church is clearly spelled out in the prophetic Scriptures. We are not left in any doubt as to what lies ahead for *this* church.

But the word "church" in the New Testament *usually* refers to what most of us think of as "*a* church"—that is, an assembly of people who call themselves Christians. The Bible speaks of the church at Corinth (1 Cor. 1:2), the churches of Galatia (Gal. 1:2), the church in the house of Nymphas (Col. 4:15), and the church in Philemon's house (Phile. 2). These "churches" are obviously local congregations in certain places.

Any definition of the church in *this* sense would probably be descriptive—it would be composed of characteristics. Not all of us would agree on which characteristics are essential, but some things are *always* true about the church as the word is used in this local sense. For one thing, it includes only living people. For another, there may be "professing" Christians in a local church—people who do not have eternal life. This was true of some in the churches to which Jude wrote (Jude 19). Actually, most people in a group could be unbelievers, and they could still call themselves a church. What lies ahead for *this* church is an entirely different question because of the spiritually mixed character of its membership.

The True Church Looks Ahead

The Bible clearly outlines the future for those who, through believing in Christ, belong to the *true* church:

1. Those in this group who die before the Lord comes will be taken immediately into His presence to be with Him forever. Their bodies will be buried, but they themselves will go immediately to heaven. To depart this life and to be with Christ is far better (Phil. 1:23), and to

be absent from the body is to be present with the Lord (2 Cor. 5:8). The bodies of these believers, whether placed in the grave the day before or hundreds of years earlier, will be raised when the Lord returns, and each will receive a new body in which he will live for all eternity. This is the prospect for those who die as members of the true church.

2. But, of course, some true believers will be living on the day Christ comes back. They will not die physically, but they will be changed, given new bodies, and taken to be with their Lord forever. We shall study this momentous event in the next chapter, for this is the event which brings to an end the history of the true church on earth.

As for Organized Religion

Most true believers do and will continue to belong to various local organized churches. Such churches are, spiritually speaking, a mixture. In their memberships are both true believers and those who merely claim to be saved. Some churches even have members who do not claim to have made a profession of faith in Christ.

What the Bible says about the future of the organized church is not encouraging. This predicted future will at that time undoubtedly be reported in both the religious and secular press.

If one were to search for a single term to describe the future of the organized church, the best term would be the word "apostasy." This will be its principal characteristic.

What is "apostasy"? The word simply means "departure." To *apostatize* is to depart from something. Such departure can be from (1) the Word of God, (2) Christian doctrine, or (3) the living God (Luke 8:13; 1 Tim. 4:1; Heb. 3:12). Apostates in the New Testament seem to be unsaved people who had made some sort of profession of faith, however shallow (2 Peter 2:1). Perhaps we could define apostasy as departure from truth which one *professed* to have accepted, or breaking a *professed* relationship with God. According to this definition, a true believer cannot apostatize, though he can be surrounded by apostasy in the organized church or denomination of which he is a part.

The three passages support our definition. In the parable of the sower, Luke 8, it seems clear that "they on the rock . . . [who] receive the Word with joy, and have no root . . . and in time of temptation fall away [apostatize]" were not genuine believers, since the test for true faith is the production of fruit, which was lacking in their cases. They *believed* (Luke 8:13), but their belief was an intellectual assent, not a fruit-bearing faith, and therefore not a saving faith (James 2:17).

False teachers are said to "depart from the faith" (1 Tim. 4:1). Whether they ever *possessed* (in contrast to *professed*) the faith is not specifically revealed in that passage. However, the false teachers described by Jude (who were evidently the first to fulfill the prophecy of 1 Timothy 4) were adjudged to be unsaved. Jude says they are without the Holy Spirit (Jude 19), and we know that "if any man have not the Spirit of Christ, he is none of His" (Rom. 8:9).

The people addressed in Hebrews 3:12 are not yet apostates but are professing church members who are being warned against the apostasy that stems from an evil heart of unbelief. The writer of Hebrews obviously believed that apostasy was a very real danger for some of his readers. He feared that some had made a profession which was not genuine, and that they would renounce it.

Lack of "fruit"—lack of love, joy, peace, patience, gentleness, goodness, faithfulness, meekness, and self-control—shows that one's experience is merely "religious" rather than life-changing (James 2:26). The fact that the readers of Hebrews are addressed as "brethren" does not necessarily show that they were genuine believers, for how else could a writer address the people of a church, even though he realized there might be unbelievers among them? The warning against apostasy was directed toward the *professing* element in the church.

Many apostates are mentioned in the Bible. For instance, Satan is an apostate. He knew the truth and deliberately departed from it (Isa.

14:12-15). The Pharisees who repudiated the Lord, though not specifically called apostates, deserve the term (Matt. 12:24). The man of sin is the climax of human apostasy (2 Thes. 2:4). Other examples of apostasy are the many disciples who went back (John 6:66), Hymenaeus and Alexander (1 Tim. 1:19-20), Demas (2 Tim. 4:10), and the false teachers of the last days (2 Peter 2:20-21).

When will apostasy occur in the organized church? The answer is always. Beyond any question, apostasy in the church is both present and future. The examples cited in the preceding paragraphs show that there were apostates in the New Testament churches. The Apostle John, writing at the close of the first century, mentioned antichrists as being actually present and active (1 John 2:18). Apostasy was present even earlier, when Paul wrote his letters to Timothy.

Apostasy plagues the church in every generation, though at the end of the church period *the* climactic apostasy will take shape, and it will lead to the religious reign of the man of sin during the Tribulation. The activities and teachings of apostates will apparently become increasingly widespread as we draw nearer to the Tribulation.

In order, therefore, to appreciate the significance of the days in which we are living, we need to do two things. First, we must learn from the Scriptures the characteristic teachings and activities of apostasy, so that we can recognize it. Then we should compare with Scripture the things being taught by religious leaders today, and survey the extent of the discrepancy, to see how near to the end of church history we are moving. In other words, we should superimpose the picture of our own day on a biblical pattern of apostasy.

Apostates Twist Truth

It will not surprise us to learn what kind of doctrine to expect in apostasy if we understand the source of such teaching, for demons inspire and promote the teachings of apostates. To be sure, apostate preachers and teachers may not realize this, but their ignorance is undoubtedly part of the satanic deception. Paul calls these teachings "doctrines of devils" (1 Tim. 4:1). It appears that the demonic spirits directly empower the antichrists as well as supply them with the source material for their teaching (1 John 4:3).

What doctrines, or teachings, characterize apostasy?

1. *Denial of the doctrine of the Trinity* (1 John 2:22-23). In John's day this denial focused on the relation between the First and Second Persons of the Trinity (the Holy Spirit did not enter the discussion). It repudiated the union of true manhood and full deity in Jesus Christ, and was a denial of the essential relations between the Father and the Son. Any nontrinitarian teaching (whether defective in relation to the Son or to the Spirit) is apostate.

2. *Denial of the incarnation of Christ* (1 John 2:22; 4:3; 2 John 7). The union of full deity and perfect humanity in the one person of Jesus Christ is a cardinal doctrine of the Christian faith, and its denial is, according to these Scriptures, a characteristic of apostasy as promoted by antichrists.

Apostates may deny either the deity of Christ or, as in John's day, the true humanity of the Son of God. Why is this so significant? Simply because the God-man is essential to the work of salvation. If the Saviour was not truly a man, He could not save, for God could not truly die. On the other hand, if the Saviour was not truly God, His death would have been to no avail. The death of a mere man cannot take away another man's sins; only God's sacrifice can do that. Therefore, the Saviour must be a God-man. The denial of this truth by apostates strikes at the heart of the Christian faith.

3. *Denial of the doctrine of the return of Christ* (2 Peter 3:4). People accept the principle of uniformitarianism—the idea that since everything has been going along in the same manner for centuries past, it will continue to go on without any direct divine intervention. Some people affirm belief in the return of Christ, but they do not mean a visible, bodily return—the sort of event that would be reported in the newspaper. That, in effect, is a denial of His return.

These are doctrines of apostasy.

False Doctrine, Low Morals

Defection in doctrine always brings a decline in morals. No passage in the Bible more vividly describes this than 2 Timothy 3:1-5. Here are listed 18 characteristics of the sort of life that apostasy promotes. Notice them as they are listed in the text:

1. love of self
2. love of money
3. a spirit of pride
4. blasphemy
5. disobedience to parents
6. lack of thankfulness
7. lack of holiness
8. lack of natural affection
9. unceasing enmity, so that men cannot be persuaded to enter into treaties with each other
10. slander
11. lack of self-control
12. savagery (the word means untamed, wild, fierce)
13. opposition to goodness
14. traitors
15. headiness (rash, headstrong, recklessness)
16. highmindedness (the word literally means to raise a smoke)
17. love of pleasure
18. a pretense of worship but without any godliness of life

The headlines of the religious sections of our news magazines read like these passages from the Bible. Liberalism has long denied the deity of Christ and the return of Christ. Now the newest fad in theology even dares to say that God Himself is both culturally irrelevant and actually dead. Jesus, if He ever did live, is not a living Person today, but is to be found in one's neighbor or in some social movement. If ever there was a more blatant denial of the Trinity, church history has failed to record it. One contemporary theologian has even said, "God is Satan."

These new theologies have one thing in common—they reject the

Bible as a proper basis of authority, and in its place substitute man's personal experience. The result of this, in the area of morals, is exactly what you might expect—every man does what seems right in his own eyes, and Paul's 18 characteristics of apostasy sound as if they were taken from today's newspaper.

The Church of Tomorrow

When the Lord comes and takes all true believers from the world, a church organization will go right on. Indeed, it will flourish. This is the church of the Tribulation. If the word "apostasy" characterizes the organized church of this day and age, the word "ecumenical" will characterize the church of that coming time.

The term "ecumenical" comes from a Greek word meaning "the inhabited world." It means *worldwide*. After true believers are taken out of the world at the rapture of the church, as we have noticed, the organized church will continue, with unbelievers leading and promoting it. This apostate church of the Tribulation will flourish, extending its influence to many peoples, multitudes, nations, and tongues (Rev. 17:15). This is why we can say it will be an ecumenical church.

To this apostate religious system, which we may be dignifying too much when we call it a church, many scholars apply the term, "Mystery, Babylon" (Rev. 17:5). Babylon was a city which had its beginnings with the building of the tower of Babel (Gen. 10:10). It flourished greatly under Nebuchadnezzar (Dan. 4:30). But in Revelation 17 "Babylon" is more than a city; it is also a system. This usage is similar to the way Americans speak of "Wall Street" or "Madison Avenue." These are actual streets, but they also stand for the financial and the advertising enterprises of this country. So Babylon stands for the religious enterprise of the Tribulation.

In addition to being ecumenical, five other characteristics are attributed to this apostate religious system called Babylon.

1. *She is called a harlot* (vv. 1, 5, 15-16). In Scripture God calls an unfaithful, flirtatious wife a harlot, the lowest of terms. This church

will claim to be connected with Christ, but will in reality be as unfaithful as a harlot. Notice again, in this instance, the basic characteristic of apostasy—the breaking of a professed relationship. Notice, too, that she is called the "great" harlot (v. 1), which distinguishes her from all the other apostate systems that have preceded her.

2. *She exercises great political power.* John saw the woman sitting on a beast, and the beast is the man of sin (Rev. 13:1-10; 17:3). By granting her favors to the kings of the earth, Babylon is able to dominate the beast, the head of the Western Federation of 10 nations (vv. 12-13). The fact that the harlot is described as sitting on the beast indicates that this religious system will dominate the political power in the West.

How could this come about? What would ever make 10 independent nations unite and then allow themselves to be dominated by a religious power? First, the allurements of the harlot will attract men. Second, men will be afraid of the great power in the area to the north of Palestine. Apparently 10 nations will be persuaded that their only defense against the Communist countries will be a religious barrier, so they will unite and then fly into the arms of the "harlot" for protection.

3. *Babylon will be a "whited sepulcher"*—inwardly corrupt and filthy, though outwardly bedecked with great glory and splendor (v. 4). It is always a temptation to think of some group other than our own as leading the trend in this direction. The truth is that several ecclesiastical groups today are guilty of attempting to cover inward infidelity to the Lord with an outward display of wealth and pomp.

4. *This system will apparently take the form of a federation* (v. 5). The harlot is also called "the mother of harlots," which seems to indicate that many groups will join in a kind of federated church organization—a number of church groups will get together under one "mother" in a kind of family relationship.

5. *The harlot religious system will persecute the true saints of God* during the Tribulation (v. 6). Though they will not belong to the

church, the body of Christ, people will be saved after the church has been raptured at the beginning of the Tribulation. Of course, these saints will not join the harlot religious system, but will be the objects of its persecution. Here will be an example of a successful attempt to make black white and white black. The apostate church (black) will sell itself to the world as the true representative of religion on the earth (white), while the saints of God (white) will be hunted down and persecuted even to death as enemies of truth (black).

These are the principal characteristics of the great religious system of the Tribulation. Three questions remain to be answered:

1. What will be the end of this system? The answer is clear: "And the 10 horns which thou sawest upon the beast, these shall hate the whore, and shall make her desolate and naked, and shall eat her flesh and burn her with fire" (Rev. 17:16). Religious Babylon, which sought out political alliances, will in the end be destroyed by the very powers that she enticed into her arms. The Western Federation of nations will revolt and destroy her completely. Most likely this will occur at the middle of the Tribulation, in order to clear the way for the head of the western nations to demand that he be worshiped.

2. Who is the mother of this harlot family? Notice two clear statements in Revelation 17. The woman sits on seven hills (v. 9), and the woman is identified as a city which reigns over the kings of earth (v. 18). In the face of these facts, some scholars associate the harlot with Rome and the religion that is headquartered there. They claim this identification is strengthened by the similarity between the religion of Babylon and the practices of Rome.

Alexander Hislop, in his book *The Two Babylons*, points out that the chief feature of the religion of Babylon was the cult of mother-child worship. This system was instituted by Nimrod's wife, Semerimus, who claimed that her son Tammuz was the fulfillment of Genesis 3:15. She symbolized this notion with the figure of a mother holding a child in her arms. Furthermore, she adopted the title "Queen of heaven" and taught that salvation was adminstered through her.

This religion appeared in one form or other in Phoenicia, Pergamos, Egypt, Greece, and Rome. It came into the experience of Israel through Jezebel and was severely condemned by the Prophet Jeremiah (44:16-19, 25). Ezekiel reveals that this evil, apostate worship had found its way into the very sanctuary of God (8:6-13).

The Roman emperor Constantine, who, like the Caesars, was the national high priest, introduced the mother-child worship cult into the Christian church when he sanctioned Christianity in A.D. 312. Pagan Romans kept right on worshiping their mother-child god and following their old rituals and holidays under the name of Christianity. This continues, under the guise of religion, to this present day. It is entirely possible that the Roman church will be the mother who takes other groups into her family to form the great apostate church of the Tribulation.

3. What is the relation to prophecy of the present ecumenical trend? The answer is not difficult. The present trend seems to be preparing the way for the final apostate religious system. The widespread character of the present apostasy in the visible church, the union of various groups into larger denominations without regard to doctrinal consideration, the increasing openness of Catholic and Protestant groups toward each other, the constant intrusion of church bodies into political affairs, and the replacing of the authority of the Bible with the presumed authority of man all seem to say very loudly that the coming of a climax is not far off.

How should a true believer react toward such truths? He should have a deep Spirit-generated compassion for those who are being deceived today into trusting a theology or an organization that cannot save. He should be increasingly burdened, while there is still time, to take the true message of life and forgiveness to those who otherwise have no hope. And, above all, he should deepen his loyalty and fidelity to the Lord who loved him enough to die for him.

7
In the
Twinkling of an Eye

The last words of a dying friend are always full of meaning, and the last words of the Lord Jesus are no exception. The scene in the Upper Room on the night of His betrayal, just before the Crucifixion, was packed with emotion. The Lord had just announced His betrayal by Judas, and His impending death (John 13:21, 31). This would involve, He said, His leaving the disciples (v. 33). As usual, Peter reacted first—in this case with a question. "Where will You go?" he asked. "And why can I not follow You, wherever it be?"

Against this background, the Bible gives us God's first revelation bearing on the tremendous event which we call the Lord's return.

There are many Christians who believe that Christ's return is one single event—that the Lord will return bodily to this earth and establish His kingdom. Many evangelical believers, however, are convinced that the Lord will return in two "stages"—that first He will return "in the air" and take His people out of the world, and that later He will return "with His saints" to set up His thousand-year kingdom. These believers refer to the first stage of Christ's coming as the "Rapture [taking away] of the church."

His Parting Promise

It is not hard to imagine the feeling that the disciples must have had when they heard that their Lord was going to leave them, and when, as far as they knew, there would never be any prospect of their seeing Him again. To comfort them, the Lord said, "In My Father's house are many mansions: if it were not so, I would have told you. I go to prepare a place for you. And if I go and prepare a place for you, I will come again, and receive you unto Myself; that where I am, there ye may be also" (John 14:2-3).

As a good bridegroom, the Lord announced His intention to prepare a dwelling place for His bride (the word *mansion* is better translated "dwelling place," like a single apartment in a large apartment complex). And, as a good bridegroom, He wants His bride with Him, so He assured the disciples that He would return to take them to be with Himself.

It is important to notice that all the Lord promised on this occasion was the simple fact that He would return for His followers—that they would see Him again. There is no elaboration of this promise. Christ did not say anything about *when* or *how* His coming would occur, but you can easily imagine what comfort He brought to the disciples, even though they could not know, at that time, all that was included in this parting promise.

A Mystery Solved

To most people, a mystery is something unintelligible—unless you know the secret of it! In Greek, the word "mystery" was used of the sacred rites of the Greek mystery religions—secrets shared only by those who had been initiated into the religion. Equivalent words in other languages sometimes indicate that a mystery is some kind of deep or high wisdom, far above finite understanding. Therefore, the word "mystery" includes the idea of something secret and of something containing deep truth.

In the New Testament, a "mystery" is a secret which has always been in the plan or purpose of God but which He has not revealed until a certain point in time.

What does this concept of a mystery have to do with the Rapture of the church? Though the Greeks believed in the immortality of the soul, they did not accept the resurrection of the body. Their thinking had affected some Christians at Corinth, so Paul wrote to them to correct their view (1 Cor. 15). He declared not only that Christ had been raised from the dead, but that all men will also someday be raised. This was not new teaching, for Christ Himself had taught the same thing. He had said that all who are in the grave will someday hear His voice and be raised, some to life and some to condemnation (John 5:26-29).

In writing to the Corinthians, Paul used the word "mystery" (1 Cor. 15:51). The work is like a red flag signaling that something hitherto unknown is about to be revealed. And the secret that is here made known is the fact that not everyone will die. The Old Testament had revealed that men would be raised from the dead (Job 19:25; Isa. 26:19; Dan. 12:2), but it had given no hint that anybody could come into God's presence without going through death and resurrection. To be sure, Enoch and Elijah had both experienced translation. That is, they had been given glorified bodies without their dying. But there was no promise that this means would be used for anyone else. That is why this newly revealed promise, "We shall not all sleep," is called a *mystery*.

A popular radio commentator, when reporting someone's death, always said, "As it must to all men, death came today to . . . . " His theology was poor, for all men will not die. There is another route into God's presence, the way of translation.

Both routes, death and translation, involve a change. Paul goes on to explain the two changes. The one will be experienced by those who have died in the Lord. Since their bodies will have seen corruption, they must put on incorruption at the resurrection of the body. But those who are living at the Lord's coming will not have died; their bodies will not have seen corruption. Therefore they will experience a different means of change. Since they will be mortal, they need only to put on immortality. This new route into God's presence is the truth that is revealed in this mystery. The dead will need resurrection, but the living will only need change (1 Cor. 15:52). God will effect this change for all living believers when the Lord comes. The last generation of Christians will not experience death.

How quickly will these two changes occur—the resurrection of dead saints and the translation of living believers? Paul says it will all happen "in a moment, in the twinkling of an eye." The whole procedure will be instantaneous, not gradual! The Greek word translated "moment" is the term from which our word *atom* comes. Because when the atom was discovered it was thought to be indivisible, it was named "atom." Even though it has been split, the term *atom* still means "indivisible." Here it indicates that the Rapture (including both dead and living saints) will take place in an indivisible instant of time.

The words "moment" and "twinkling" refer to the instantaneous nature of this event, and the phrase "at the last trump" reminds us of its finality. After the trumpet sounds, there will be no time to prepare, for the changes will occur instantly. There will be no second chance for those who, up till then, have refused the grace of God.

Paul says we shall *all* be changed in that instant. This would seem to disprove the teaching that only certain believers will be raptured, while others will be left to go through a partial rapture.

To sum up: expanding on the Lord's promise to come again, Paul revealed (1 Cor. 15:51-57) four features of this event: (1) It will include not only the bodily resurrection of those believers who have died, but also the changing of the bodies of those who are alive at the time it happens. (2) It will be instantaneous. (3) It will be final. (4) It will include *all* believers, not simply *some* of them.

None Left Out

As in the church at Corinth, there was a problem in the church at Thessalonica, too. Early Christians in Thessalonica, like those elsewhere, expected the Lord to return within their lifetime, but He did not. In time, some of them died. Those who remained thought that those who died had been robbed of sharing in the glorious reign of Christ. Paul's answer to the problem is a reassuring affirmation that the dead will certainly be raised and will therefore share in the kingdom. The apostle gives a detailed picture of this resurrection of believers, including the change that will at the same time take place in living believers.

Our assurance that all this will happen is based on our hope of sharing in the resurrection of Christ (vv. 13-14) and on the direct promise of the Word of the Lord (v. 15).

The certainty of a Christian's resurrection is based on the fact of Christ's rising. When the word "sleep," in the New Testament, is used of death, it is used only in relation to the death of believers—never of unbelievers. The object of this metaphor is to suggest that as a sleeper does not cease to exist while his body sleeps, so a dead believer continues to exist even if those who remain alive cannot communicate with him. Moreover, sleep is temporary, and so is the death of the body. Sleep ends in waking, death in resurrection.

Any sorrow which a Christian may have over the loss of a loved one (and it is comforting to remember that our Lord wept when His friend Lazarus died, John 11:33-35) is unlike the hopeless despair which unbelievers have.

Actually, Paul did *not* really say that Christians may sorrow, only not to the same degree as the heathen, for such an interpretation would strain the words, "even as." He said that Christians are *not* like the heathen because Christians *do not* sorrow. He did not deny that we grieve over loss (Phil. 2:27), but that is not the point here.

Our assured hope is based on our preview of resurrection, as seen in the resurrection of Christ. The "if" (1 Thes. 4:14) does not express doubt, and it may be translated "since." The resurrection of Christ *guarantees* the resurrection of Christians.

By contrast, here is an example of the hopelessness of the heathen in the face of death, from a letter written in the second century: "Eirene to Taonnophris and Philon, good cheer! I was as much grieved and shed as many tears over Eumoiros as I shed for Didymas, and I did everything that was fitting, and so did my whole family . . . but still there is nothing one can do in the face of such trouble. So I leave you to comfort yourselves. Good-bye."

After the preview comes a promise (v. 15), and the statement is made as authoritative as possible by the declaration that it is the Word of the Lord. Another detail is added: the dead will have first place. At the Lord's coming, those who are living will not precede those who have died. Paul included himself ("we") among the living group. Evidently he expected to live until the return of Christ. This is one of the wonderful things about the hope of Christ's coming—it is equally bright for each generation, regardless of how long it seems to be delayed.

What will happen when the Lord returns? Five features are spotlighted:

1. *Christ will return* (v. 16). He Himself, not an emissary or agent whom He might send in His place, will come for His people. Because He Himself will come, the attendant circumstances will include all the grandeur His personal presence deserves.

There will be a shout. This word of command is used in classical Greek for the shout with which an officer gave the order to his troops or his crew. There is in the term a ring of authority and a note of urgency. It is not said who utters the shout—whether it is the Lord or an archangel—but the voice of an archangel will be heard. Michael is the only archangel mentioned in the Bible by name (Jude 9), but it is not impossible that there are other archangels (see Daniel 10:13). The trumpet of God will also sound when Christ comes—a detail already noticed (1 Cor. 15:52).

2. *There will be a resurrection* (v. 16). Again the priority of the dead is mentioned. They will be raised before those who are alive are changed. All will happen, however, in the twinkling of an eye. The group raised at this time is limited to those who are "in Christ." This indicates that not all the dead will be raised at the same time. The passage does not support the idea, so often heard, of a "general resurrection." At this point, only dead *believers* will be made alive.

3. *The Rapture will occur* (v. 17). Living believers will be changed and "caught up to be with the Lord." The word "caught up" means to "seize" or to "snatch," and this verb, in Latin is the term from which we get the English word "rapture." Strictly speaking, the word *rapture* means the act of conveying a person from one place to

another, and is properly used of the taking of living persons to heaven. Paul used it of his own experience of being caught up into the third heaven (2 Cor. 12:4). However, we use the term "rapture of the church" loosely to include all that happens at Christ's coming, including not only the change in living Christians but also the resurrection of dead believers. The term "rapture" implies whatever change is necessary to fit mortal bodies for immortal existence in heaven. Though the method of this change is nowhere explained, Paul clearly believed that it is possible to have such a metamorphosis without Christians experiencing the dissolution caused by death and the grave.

4. *There will be a reunion* (v. 17), and it will be twofold. Living Christians will be reunited with loved ones who have died, for they shall be caught up together with them. But even more wonderful will be the reunion of the church with the Lord. Both these reunions will be forever!

5. *This truth is a constant reassurance to all believers* (v. 18). They need not sorrow over those who have died. Comfort and hope are the logical consequences of this glorious truth.

We often hear of the "secret rapture." This term is misleading, for though the time of the event is unknown, the effects will be openly observed anywhere there were Christians before its occurrence. Newspaper headlines and radio and TV reports on the news will "cover" this event, or at least the results of it. Some places will be almost or entirely unaffected by the removal of living Christians because there will be few or no believers there.

It is rather intriguing to speculate on what explanation TV commentators will give on the day the Rapture takes place. Undoubtedly they will try to give "rational" and "reasonable" appraisals that leave the Bible out. However, some people will remember hearing the Rapture preached on, or will turn to their Bibles and read God's explanation. But no matter how people will try to explain it, the event will happen just as God, in His prophetic Word, has said it will.

They Don't Agree on the "When"

We have seen that there are several views concerning the time of the Lord's coming in relation to the Millennium. There are also differing viewpoints about the relation between His coming for the church and the time of the Tribulation, though this question is generally discussed only among premillenarians. Amillenarians believe there is only one future and final coming of Christ, followed immediately by the ushering in of eternity. Postmillennialists do not believe in a tribulation period at all, and in their view, Christ comes after the Millennium is over.

Premillennialists agree that at the conclusion of a time of tribulation on this earth (most concur that this period will be seven years long) the Lord will return and establish His millennial kingdom. They also agree that His coming for His own people is described as distinct and separate from His Second Coming. They disagree on *when* His coming for His own people will occur in relation to His second return to earth to set up His kingdom.

Posttribulationists say that Christ's coming *for* His saints and His coming *with* His saints will both occur in quick succession after the Tribulation. They would chart their viewpoint as shown in figure 9.

Midtribulationists believe that Christ's coming for His people will happen at the middle point of the Tribulation period—that is, three and a half years before the time when the Lord returns with His people to set up His kingdom. Diagrammed, their idea is like that shown in figure 10 on page 86.

Pretribulationists hold that the coming of Christ for His people will take place before the Tribulation begins at all, and that the church will escape the entire period of trouble here on the earth. Then, seven years later, after the Tribulation concludes, the Lord will return to earth with His redeemed people to set up His kingdom. Pretribulationism looks like that shown in figure 11 on page 87.

Those who believe in the pretribulation view of the Rapture support their position with two principal reasons:

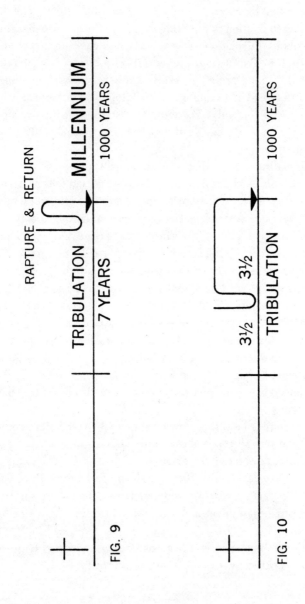

FIG. 9

RAPTURE & RETURN

TRIBULATION

MILLENNIUM

7 YEARS

1000 YEARS

FIG. 10

3½

3½

TRIBULATION

1000 YEARS

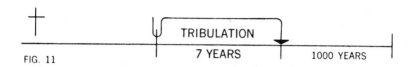

FIG. 11

1. The risen Lord promised the church at Philadelphia to "keep thee from the hour of temptation, which shall come upon all the world, to try them that dwell upon the earth" (Rev. 3:10). They apply this promise, like promises made in other letters to local churches, to the whole church (though obviously it will be experienced only by believers living when Christ comes), and they assume that the "hour of temptation" refers to the Tribulation.

Some people say this promise merely means that Christians will be protected from the plagues and persecutions of the Tribulation, though they will live *through* it—much as the Children of Israel were kept from the effects of some of the plagues in Egypt though they lived through them. But, of course, the promise is not only to keep *from* (and the preposition means *from,* not *in*) the trouble, but to keep from the *hour* (or time) of trouble. The promise to be kept from the hour of trouble would seem to imply exemption from being anywhere around when it took place. Since the Tribulation will be worldwide, such exemption could be given to living believers only by removing all of them from the earth before the trouble begins.

2. The Tribulation is called "the great day of His wrath" (Rev. 6:17). Believers, who know the Deliverer from the wrath to come (1 Thes. 1:10), are assured that God has not appointed them to wrath (5:9). Since in the context of this latter verse Paul is speaking about the *beginning* of the Tribulation period (5:2), it seems clear that he is saying that Christians will not be present during any part of the time of wrath, but will be removed before it begins. The pretribulation view seems to be more compatible with the concept of the Rapture as a comforting and blessed hope.

It Could Be Today

I believe that the Rapture of believers can occur at any time. Nothing is yet unfulfilled which must take place before believers are caught up to meet the Lord in the air.

There are two indications that the Rapture may be very close. One is the increase of apostasy in the organized church in the world today. We saw in chapter 6 some details of the apostasy which characterize the church in this age. Since these evidences seem to be increasing, we may say that the Rapture is nearer. They are in fact sufficiently present in the church today that one wonders how they could increase much before the Lord comes.

Apostasy is characteristic of the church throughout all of its history; increasing apostasy is a significant sign of the rapidly approaching end of human history as we know it.

We may also realize the nearness of His coming by comparing the Bible picture of times during the pretribulation days with conditions as they are today. If the trends, apostasy, alliances, and other characteristics of the Tribulation seem to be similar to those which exist today, we may safely conclude that the Tribulation is probably not far off. And if it is near, then so is the coming of the Lord. We shall learn more of these details in the next two chapters and compare our own times with God's picture of the future.

By every indication which we can gauge, the Rapture seems near. Certainly each day that passes brings it 24 hours nearer, and each trend that develops points to its coming. God says that this is a blessed hope—at least it *will* be if we are ready to meet the Lord. If not, we should *get* ready and then know the joy of eagerly anticipating seeing Him whose coming will be "in the twinkling of an eye."

8
The Next Seven Years

The next seven years? Yes, the seven years after the momentous event we studied in the last chapter. The Scriptures describe in detail the events that will take place on earth after the church has been taken to heaven. These events will appear in the headlines of whatever newspapers are published during the Tribulation, and they will not make pleasant reading.

Nothing Like It

In describing the tribulation period, the Lord said it will be a time "such as was not since the beginning of the world to this time, no, nor ever shall be" (Matt. 24:21). It will be a time of trouble unique in the history of the world. There have been many difficult times since the Lord spoke these words, and He Himself warned the disciples, "In the world ye shall have tribulation" (John 16:33). What is it, then, that makes this future period different? How will it be unique?

Two characteristics will distinguish the Tribulation from all other hard times that the world has seen. First, it will be worldwide, not localized, as stated in the promise of deliverance already noted (Rev. 3:10) and as described in detail in the judgments of the Revelation. The intense local persecutions and calamities of this present day cannot be the beginning of the Tribulation, for that time will affect *the entire world*.

Then, too, the Tribulation will be unique because of the way men act. In one of the early judgments, men will hide themselves in the dens and caves of the mountains and say, "Fall on us, and hide us from the face of Him that sitteth on the throne, and from the wrath of the

Lamb" (Rev. 6:16). When the Great Tribulation comes, men will act as if they think the world is coming to an end.

For years some men have been talking as if they *thought* the end were near, but at the beginning of the Tribulation they will *realize* that the end is actually at hand. Scientists, politicians, and even church leaders warn today that the end of human history could be upon us, and even use the term "Armageddon," but people are not behaving as if they believed it. Real estate is being bought and sold, savings are being accumulated, and plans are continually being made for the future. But when the Tribulation comes, people will hide in bomb shelters and will actually seek death rather than try to preserve life. The future, in those days, will hold no attraction.

The uniqueness of the Tribulation lies in its being worldwide and in its terror, which will cause men to want to die rather than live.

What We'll Do

In this chapter and the next one we want to try to present the picture of the Tribulation as chronologically accurate as possible. The sequence cannot, of course, be exact, and all scholars will not always agree with the interpretation given in this course.

Generally, if the Tribulation were likened to a seven-layer cake, one layer for each year, the study procedure would be to slice the cake down, subject by subject. Thus there would be a slice of Antichrist, a slice of Jewish history, a slice of the wrath of God, a slice of Satan, and so forth. By contrast, using the same illustration, we shall assimilate the cake layer by layer—that is, year by year. This process will help you understand what events will happen as the period goes on.

First Signs of Trouble

The Tribulation does not necessarily begin the day the church is taken to meet the Lord in the air. Though I believe that the Rapture precedes the beginning of the Tribulation, actually nothing is said in the Scriptures as to whether or not some time (or how much time) may elapse between the Rapture and the opening of the Tribulation.

The Tribulation actually begins with the signing of a covenant between the leader of the "Federated States of Europe" and the Jewish people. This treaty will set in motion the events of the 70th week (or seven years) of Daniel's prophecy, studied in chapter 2. We noticed, there, that there is an interval of undetermined length between the first 69 weeks of seven years each and the last or 70th week of seven years.

We are living in that interval. It is the time in which God is forming the church, the body of Christ, by saving Jews and Gentiles alike. Since God has not yet finished this present program, the last week of the 70 has not yet begun. When it does, God will once again turn His attention in a special way to His people the Jews, and to His holy city Jerusalem, as outlined in Daniel 9:24.

When this last period of 7 years begins, "he shall confirm the convenant with many for one week" (Dan. 9:27). Who does the "he" refer to? Grammatically it could refer either to Messiah (v. 26) or to "the prince who shall come," who will probably be related to the people who destroyed Jerusalem in A.D. 70. The latter view is better, because usually the antecedent nearer to a pronoun is preferred, and in this case it is the prince, not Messiah. Then, too, nothing in the record of Christ's life in any way connects Him with the making (and later breaking) of a seven-year covenant with the Jewish people.

We have already met this man. He is the "little horn" (Dan. 7:24-25) who heads the coalition of western nations in the Tribulation days. He is also called the "man of sin" (2 Thes. 2:3), and is referred to as the beast (Rev. 11:7; 13:1; 17:11; 19:20). At the beginning of the Tribulation he will make a covenant, or enter a league, with Israel. This treaty will align the West with the Jewish nation and will guarantee protection to Israel so that she may reestablish the ancient rituals of Judaism. It appears that this provision will also assure protection while Israel rebuilds the temple in Jerusalem as the center of her religious observances. Since we know that the covenant will be broken and the man of sin will be worshiped in the temple of God, obviously a temple will have been already built during the first part of the Tribulation (2 Thes. 2:4).

The alignment of western Europe with Israel is interesting in the light of current events. It seems to indicate that Israel will not of herself be sufficiently strong to feel secure in the face of the hostile states around her. She will not be able to "go it alone" at this point, and so will form an alliance with the western nations. Then the outlook for Israel will seem bright. She will feel secure in her land; she will be worshiping according to the Old Testament pattern; she will have a temple again in Jerusalem; and she will be important among the nations of the world. But this is only the beginning.

Seals, Trumpets, and Bowls

Revelation 6—19 describes the Tribulation in detail. We read here about three series of judgments. The first series is related to the opening of the seven seals of a scroll, the second to the blowing of seven trumpets, and the third to the pouring out of the contents of seven bowls.

Do these three series of judgments follow each other in succession, or do the trumpets and the bowls recapitulate the judgments of the seals with greater intensity? In other words, do the trumpet and bowl judgments follow the seals as different and distinct judgments, or do they picture the same judgments?

I believe the three series follow one another in chronological sequence and that there is no recapitulation. Either way, however, the seal judgments are the first judgments of the tribulation days, and will probably occur during the first year of that period.

The First Seal Judgment (Rev. 6:1-2). The opening of the first seal revealed to John a white horse ridden by one who went forth conquering. In interpreting the Revelation, always begin with what is the clearest. Here, it is quite obvious that the opening months of the Tribulation will see nations conquered by the rider on the horse. Some think this rider is the man of sin, the head of the western coalition of nations. His method of conquest, however, we would call "cold" war. Clearly, this description coincides exactly with the picture of the beginning of the Tribulation given in 1 Thessalonians 5:3—it will be a day when men are talking about peace and safety. This may indicate that we are living in the days immediately preceding the Tribulation—but, on the other hand, there is nothing in the Word of God which would indicate that there could not be another world war in this present age, then *another* time of peace before the Lord comes. Other evangelical scholars agree that the first rider simply represents the spirit of conquest—an attitude that has characterized the nations throughout human history. Doubtless this spirit will be intensified as the end approaches.

The Second Seal Judgment (Rev. 6:3-4). In the judgment of the second seal, peace will be removed from the earth and men will war with each other. The phrase, "there was given unto him a great sword," confirms this interpretation. The red color of the second horse suggests bloodshed. War has always followed the spirit of conquest.

The Third Seal Judgment (Rev. 6:5-6). The third judgment (still probably in the first year of the Tribulation) brings famine to the world. A black horse pictures this event, and the pair of balances carried by his rider bespeaks a careful rationing of food. A "penny" (v. 6), the Roman denarius, was a day's wages in Palestine in Jesus' day (Matt. 20:2). Normally, it would buy eight measures of wheat or 24 of barley. Under the famine conditions of these coming days, a day's wage will buy only one measure of wheat or three of barley—one eighth the normal supply of food. However, there is an ironic twist to this famine. Oil and wine, the very things a majority of people cannot afford, will not be in short supply. The scarcity of basic foods and the availability of luxury items will taunt the common people in their impoverished state.

The Fourth Seal Judgment (Rev. 6:7-8). This horse will be, literally, a yellowish green. He is the only horseman who is named, and he is called Death. Death, of course, claims the physical part of man, and it is accompanied by Hades, the place of the dead (v. 8), which claims the immaterial part. The effect of this judgment will be devastating—one fourth of earth's population will be killed by the sword (war), by hunger (the famine that often accompanies war), by death (perhaps by the plagues and diseases that follow war), and by wild beasts of the earth, which apparently will be unrestrained at this time and will roam about freely, killing men. Man's cleverly devised schemes for bringing in peace, plenty, and longevity will be overturned in the short space of time this judgment will take.

The Fifth Seal Judgment (Rev. 6:9-11). Though the action of the fifth seal is in heaven, it presupposes that certain events have happened on earth. The group of martyrs in heaven (v. 9) implies that these people have already been killed on earth, early in the Tribulation. These people will be witnessing for Christ early in the Tribulation. They will be slain because of their testimony.

The Sixth Seal Judgment (Rev. 6:12-17). This judgment unleashes universal havoc on the earth. It will include six catastrophic events: (1) A single great earthquake will take place. (2) The sun will be darkened so that it becomes black as sackcloth. The text does not say that the sun will be turned into sackcloth, but that it will be blackened *as* sackcloth. (3) The moon will become as red *as* blood. (4) There will be a meteor shower, with all the natural devastating consequences that follow. (5) Apparently heaven will be opened for a moment so that the men on earth can have a glimpse of that awesome scene, with God on His throne. (6) Every mountain and island will be moved.

These judgments will produce terror in the hearts of all living men. Their hearts will be filled with fear—not primarily because of the physical disturbances or the awful wars and pestilences, but because they will see God on His throne. Men will plead to be hidden "from the face of Him that sitteth on the throne, and from the wrath of the Lamb." They will go to any length to avoid facing their Creator and Judge, even to seeking death under the rocks and mountains in which they will try to hide. All classes of people (v. 15) will be affected. As has been true throughout history, there will be no *general* or mass turning *to* God in repentance, but only a turning *from* God's face.

These will be the first judgments of the Tribulation. But these will be only the beginning—the worst is yet to come.

Religion on the Skids

We have already learned two things about the religion of tribulation days. We have studied, in chapter 6, the rise to power of the great ecumenical church in the first three and one half years of the Tribulation. During this time, this church will be at her zenith, sitting on the beast (Rev. 17:3) and exerting tremendous political power in the affairs of nations.

The second thing we have learned is that by the time of the fifth seal a number of true believers will have been martyred. In other words, during the first years of the Tribulation there will be a true witness to the Gospel, and this will be opposed by the ecumenical church, which will be "drunken with the blood of the saints, and with the blood of the martyrs of Jesus" (Rev. 17:6). In the name of religion, the organized church of the first part of the Tribulation will kill true believers for their faith.

But a piece of the puzzle is missing. How will these true believers have been converted in the first place? With the Rapture of the church, all Christians will have been removed from earth, so that none will be alive immediately after the Rapture. If there are to be martyrs, there must first be believers. How will men be saved? In Revelation 7:1-8, we are introduced to a sort of parenthesis in judgment. Even the wind does not blow. (Incidentally, can you imagine the effect on climate of the cessation of the wind even for a short time? Add the disturbance in the topography of the earth, with the shifting of islands and mountains, and you can begin to grasp the increased chaos during these early years of the Tribulation.)

The purpose of this suspension of judgment is that a certain group of people may be "sealed" (7:3). These people are called "the servants of our God." Why they are is described in detail in verses 4-8. They are Jews from each of the 12 tribes, and they do some particular service for God. Whether the seal placed on them is a visible mark or characteristic of some kind is neither stated nor implied in the text. A seal need not be visible to be real (Eph. 4:30). It is principally a guarantee of ownership and security. Both these ideas are involved in the sealing of this group. These people are owned by God, which means that they are redeemed. They are kept secure by God, which may mean He protects them from their enemies on earth while they complete their service for Him.

But how were these people saved? Even though there will be no Christians on earth immediately after the Rapture, there will be Bibles, and books about the Christian faith. In other words, information will be available to give men the facts on which to find saving faith.

What will be the important work for which God will protect these people supernaturally? Actually, this passage does not specify, but we have hints as to the answer in Revelation 14, where the same group is described as in heaven after their work has been completed. They are said to be the redeemed followers of the Lamb, which may indicate that they are a group of special witnesses to the Gospel in the tribulation days. They will not be the only ones witnessing, but they will be the only group given special protection from their enemies.

The first judgments of the Tribulation, and the religious situation in the first part of that period, are repeated, in summary form, in the Lord's Olivet discourse (Matt. 24). Verses 4-14 cover the events of the first half of the Tribulation, for at verse 15 we read about an event that occurs exactly halfway through the seven-year period. Notice how the seal judgments are summarized: "And ye shall hear of wars and rumors of wars . . . for nation shall rise against nation, and kingdom against kingdom; and there shall be famines, and pestilences, and earthquakes in divers places" (vv. 6-7). Notice the reference to the martyrs of the fifth seal: "Then shall they deliver you up to be afflicted and shall kill you" (v. 9). Look at the false religion: "And many false prophets shall rise and shall deceive many" (v. 11). The ministry of the 144,000 sealed ones, and other witnesses, will account for "this Gospel of the Kingdom shall be preached in all the world for a witness unto all nations" (v. 14). Here are all the major events of the first half of the Tribulation, in capsule form, from Christ's lips before the Crucifixion.

Egypt a Threat to Palestine

So far, in these studies, we have focused our attention chiefly on the western federation of nations, headed by the man of sin. But during the first part of the Tribulation other powerful alliances will exist or be in the making. Egypt, to the south of Palestine, will continue to be a strong and threatening nation until the man of sin conquers her. This defeat is predicted in Daniel 11:40-43, and though scholars do not agree as to when this will occur, it seems to be no later than the middle of the Tribulation.

So we can expect to see Egypt remain a power to be reckoned with until about three years of the Tribulation have elapsed. Then, she will be defeated and looted by the "Federated States of Europe", which had entered into a defense pact with her. Egypt does not figure in any of the power blocs or wars of the last half of the Tribulation.

The nations of the East will be forming some sort of coalition and will not actively take part in any of the events involving Palestine until the very end of the Tribulation. All trends among eastern nations toward independence and detachment from western influence are significant. They may be preparatory to the alliance that those nations will form.

By far the most important bloc, besides the western confederation of nations, is that of Gog and Magog. The names listed in Ezekiel 38; 39 are identified in Genesis 10:2 as sons of Japheth. The Japhethites migrated, after the Flood, from Asia Minor to the north, beyond the Caspian and Black Seas. They settled in the area we know today as modern Russia. "Gog" and "Magog," therefore, may refer to the people who live north of Palestine in Russia. She will have with her as allies Persia (modern Iran), Ethiopia (northern Sudan), Put (Libya), Gomer (probably the eastern part of Turkey and the Ukraine), and Togarmah (the part of Turkey near the Syrian border) (Ezek. 38:5-6).

The West will lodge a protest (Ezek. 38:13), but to no avail, and this invading army from the north will cover Israel like a cloud (v. 16). These soldiers will go to rob and plunder the land which thought it was safe under the protection of the West.

At this point God will step in and utterly destroy the forces of Russia and her allies (Ezek. 38:21—39:7). The seemingly invincible troops will be supernaturally defeated and completely routed. The Russian army will be buried in Israel (Ezek. 39:11), and only then will Russian influence in the Middle East be ended—by the direct intervention of God.

If we are living today near the Rapture of the church and the beginning of the Tribulation, we may expect to see certain trends in relation to the nation: Israel. (1) Her ties with the West will develop and grow stronger, until at the beginning of the Tribulation Israel and the West will conclude a mutual assistance treaty. (2) We will see Egypt continue to be an independent and important nation. (3) Russia will continue to influence the Middle East, most likely through the Arab states of that area. (4) The climax will be an invasion of Palestine, for since Israel will choose to align herself with the West, this will be the only way Russia can take her over. But God will intervene and will bring a spectacular judgment on Russia, resulting in her complete defeat. Godless, atheistic Communism will end in this ignominious way.

When will this happen? This is not an easy question to answer, but it is probable that the conquest of Egypt and the defeat of Russia will both occur just before the middle of the Tribulation. This will clear the way for the man of sin to assert himself as a world ruler, which would seem impossible if the king of the north (Russia) were still a mighty power opposing him.

These events will make startling headlines in whatever newspapers will be printed in those awful days. Have you ever wondered how the world leaders will explain some of these events? How will they explain the changes in climate? What will be their answer to famine and pestilence? How will they justify the need for another war here and yet another one there? With "managed news," censored reports, and even the organized church blessing their pronouncements, their explanations may sound quite plausible. Add the huge amounts of money they will pour into disaster areas, and long debates in the United Nations, and you have the salve which will deceive some men into thinking that they are still masters of their own fate and designers of their own destiny.

Will men see their need of a Saviour and turn to Him in repentance? There will be a witness to the truth, and some will heed it, but most men will harden their hearts against God and His provision for eternal life.

Such will be life in the first half of the Tribulation. It is not a pleasant prospect, but the worst is yet to come.

Climax of ⁹Judgment

The Scriptures often divide the seven years of the Tribulation into two equal parts. The last of Daniel's 70 "weeks" of seven years is divided in the middle by a significant event (Dan. 9:27). In the Revelation the two halves of the Tribulation are designated either by "time, times, and half a time" (12:14), or "42 months" (11:2; 13:5), or "1,260 days" (11:3; 12:6), each of which intervals works out to 3½ years.

Though one cannot always be certain about the chronology of the mentioned events, many of them can be pinpointed with reasonable accuracy in the tribulation period. In the previous chapter, we surveyed the first three and a half years of the period. We are now at the midpoint of the seven-year Tribulation.

Antichrist on the Loose

With the invasion of Palestine from the north by Gog and Magog, it may seem for a time that the plans of the man of sin (Antichrist) are almost crushed. But supernatural intervention by God and the destruction of the Russian hordes will clear the way for the beast to resume his scheming. First, however, he must eliminate opposition from two individuals (Rev. 11:3-13) who have been plaguing him. The killing of these "two witnesses" will be the beast's first great feat at the middle of the Tribulation.

The two witnesses will have a spectacular ministry during the first part of the Tribulation. They will have power to kill their enemies with fire, to prevent rain, to turn water to blood, and to bring plagues on the earth as often as they wish. Their frequent use of these powers will add to the general devastation. Think, for instance, what will happen when they use their power to prevent rain. Along with the climatic and topographical changes that will occur on earth, unimaginable disaster will result.

Though the witnesses will be invincible for three and a half years, God will permit the beast to kill them after they have finished their work (v. 7). Making martyrs of the witnesses will win Antichrist wide support among the people of the world. But he will not be satisfied with merely killing them; he will display their bodies in the streets of Jerusalem. People, seeing the witnesses dead, will rejoice that they will no longer have to hear their warnings.

Merely to look on the decaying bodies of these two men will not satisfy people. They will make a great holiday of the occasion, and will send gifts to each other. Interestingly enough, this is the only occasion, during the entire tribulation period, on which rejoicing is mentioned. People will be so overjoyed that the witnesses are dead that this will be a happy holiday for them. If they had believed the witnesses' preaching, their deaths would have been a sad occasion instead of a holiday.

But God will intervene. After three and a half days, the bodies of the two witnesses will be resurrected and translated into heaven in a cloud of glory. Imagine the scene. Long lines will be waiting to view the corpses. Perhaps the cameras will be focusing on them at the very moment of their resurrection. People in Europe and America will be watching via satellite transmission. The calm, matter-of-fact announcer will suddenly become nearly hysterical as he sees a resurrection in process and realizes that millions of people are depending on him for an explanation. How will the interpreters of the news manage this one? Even the voice from heaven (v. 12) will be heard in millions of homes.

But even before the newspapers can report the story or the commentators write their analyses, there will be another great event for them to cover, an earthquake which will center in Jerusalem and which will destroy a tenth part of the city, killing 7,000 people.

At this time too, apparently, the 144,000 witnesses (Rev. 7) will also be killed, and the beast will destroy the ecumenical church (Rev. 17:16) to clear away opposition to his next great act.

Having rid himself of all religious opposition, the beast will issue an edict: "Worship me." To enforce his command he will have to break his treaty with the Jews which allowed them to restore Jewish worship in their rebuilt temple at Jerusalem. This he will do (Dan. 9:27), demanding that he be the object of all worship (Matt. 24:15; 2 Thes. 2:4).

How will he accomplish this?

First of all, he will have superhuman help. Satan, we are told, will give him his power and throne and great authority (Rev. 13:2). The devil will work furiously, from this point on, to do everything in his power to thwart God's plans. He will make war with Michael and his angels—and lose. This will result in his being cast out of heaven. Then God will warn the inhabitants of the earth, "Woe . . . for the devil is come down unto you, having great wrath, because he knoweth that he hath but a short time" (Rev. 12:12). The power of Satan will be behind the acts of the beast, Antichrist, and he will use him to the full.

Another reason for the beast's greatness involves his being wounded unto death. His deadly wound will be healed (13:3), so that all the world will wonder. The phrase, "wounded to death," literally means, "as having been slain to death," and it is exactly the same phrase as is used in Revelation 5:6 in reference to the death of Christ.

Since Christ actually died, perhaps the beast also will actually die and then be restored to life. He is said to rise out of the abyss (11:7), which seems to confirm the idea that he experiences a resurrection. If not, the text at least means he will have some kind of spectacular restoration so that the world will wonder after him. His miraculous resurrection or restoration will make all men acknowledge his uniqueness ("Who is like unto the beast?") and his might ("Who is able to make war with him?")

The beast's program will include blasphemy and war (13:5-7). He will speak insolently against God (Dan. 7:25). Objects of his blasphemy will include the name of God, the dwelling place of God, and those who dwell in heaven. He will be allowed (notice that God is still in control) to make war with the saints (Rev. 12:17), and to kill them. But his power will be limited by God to 42 months.

Here is an example of the interweaving of the many forces behind events: God will control all, but Satan will empower the beast, who in turn will act on his own in blaspheming God. Men who join his army and fight for him will do so voluntarily, and they in turn will make martyrs of God's people who, though they are killed, will still be within God's protecting care!

In order to promote his program more efficiently, Antichrist will have an important lieutenant. He is the "second beast" (13:11-18), and his sole duty is to promote the purposes and expedite the worship of the first beast, the man of sin. At no time in his career does beast No. 2 promote himself, but his concerns are always centered in the first beast. His power will be as great as that of the man of sin, but he will use it in the interests of his superior, not for himself (13:12).

This lieutenant will be able to make fire come down on the earth, duplicating the power of the two witnesses in order to show the world that he is as great as they were (v. 13). He will be able to work other miracles (vv. 13-14). He will order men to make an image of the first beast (v. 14), and apparently they will do it willingly and quickly. His next step will be to give life to the image they have made. The word for "life" (v. 15) is *pneuma, spirit,* and this could indicate a supernatural miracle (empowered by Satan) which will actually give life to the image. Of course, the word may be translated "wind," which may indicate some magical sleight of hand, on the part of the lieutenant, to give the image the appearance of real life. The speech and movement of an image could easily be artificial, but they could with equal ease be the work of Satan.

However, the greatest feat of the second beast, who is sometimes called "the false prophet" (16:13; 19:20; 20:10), will be a squeeze play on men to force them to worship the man of sin. It will be a simple scheme, cleverly devised: "And he causeth all, both small and great, rich and poor, free and bond, to receive a mark in their right hand, or in their foreheads: and that no man might buy or sell, save he that had the mark, or the name of the beast, or the number of his name" (13:16-17). In other words: bow or starve.

A "mark" is an impression made by a stamp, such as a brand used on slaves and animals. Men will become slaves of the man of sin and will have to bear the identifying mark of their slavery. Perhaps timid slaves will have the mark placed in their right hands. To avoid embarrassment, they may try to avoid shaking hands with people in order to conceal the mark. Bold followers of Antichrist may have the mark placed in the middle of their foreheads.

What will this mark be like? Verse 17 indicates that it will be either the name of the beast or his number, and the number is further explained as 666, the number of the man of sin, *not* of his lieutenant. This number has been linked to so many personages as to make them all unreliable coincidences. When this great ruler comes to power, however, there will be no mistake as to who he is. In some way unknown to us now, the number 666 will play a principal part in his identification (Rev. 16:13; 19:20; 20:10).

This will be a grim time in the history of the world. I suppose that Antichrist would succeed completely in bringing the entire world to his feet were it not for the presence of the godly remnant, who will refuse to bow, and for the shortness of the time available to him.

Judgment and More of It

In the meantime, God will continue to pour out the judgments of His wrath on the earth. The first series of judgments will be unleashed as the seals of a book are opened. We have already seen what will happen as the first six seals are broken. With the opening of the seventh seal (Rev. 8:1) one would expect a holocaust to let loose. Instead, there is silence—the still silence of expectancy and foreboding. The silence will last for half an hour and will be awesome. The opening of this seventh seal introduces another series of judgments which are announced by the blowing of seven trumpets (8:7—9:21; 11:15-19). The last three of the seven trumpet judgments are distinguished from the first four by being specially designated as "woes" which seems to imply that they are of harsher character.

Where is the middle (three-and-a-half-year) point of the Tribulation in relation to these judgments? The Scriptures do not specifically say, but many feel that the middle point comes either with the first trumpet judgment or with the first woe judgment (which is the fifth trumpet judgment). If this is so, the first trumpet judgment comes about when Antichrist kills the two witnesses and sets himself up to be worshiped. The trumpet judgments seem to continue on into the last year of the period. They are followed by a final rapid series of further judgments in the last months of the seventh year.

The First Trumpet Judgment (Rev. 8:7) will rain hail, and fire, mingled with blood, on the earth, so that a third part of the earth, trees, and grass will be burned. Fire and blood, here, are not symbols of something else. We are to take them literally. They will devastate vegetation on the earth and further add to the climatic disruptions.

The Second Trumpet Judgment (Rev. 8:8-9) is explained with a figure of speech—"*as it were* a great mountain burning with fire." Probably nothing in the realm of our present experience corresponds to this. It will likely be something about which we do not yet know anything, but its effect is clear—a third part of the sea will become blood, and a third part of the world's shipping will be destroyed. Think of how this judgment will affect the headlines of the papers and the hearts of the people.

The Third Trumpet Judgment (Rev. 8:10-11) will pollute the world's fresh water supply so that many will die.

The Fourth Trumpet Judgment (Rev. 8:12-13) will affect the sun, moon, stars, and the uniformity of the day-night cycle. Since one third of the heavenly bodies will be smitten, perhaps the 24-hour cycle of day and night will be shortened to 16 hours. The Lord Jesus predicted, in His Olivet discourse, "signs in the sun, and in the moon, and in the stars" (Luke 21:25).

The First Woe—the Fifth Trumpet Judgment (Rev. 9:1-2). Like arrows from a bow, the locusts of this first woe judgment will be discharged upon earth. They originate from the bottomless pit—literally, from the "shaft of the abyss." This pit, entered by a shaft, is under lock and key. Incidentally, Revelation 9 contains more occurrences of the words "as" and "like" than any other chapter in the Bible. It was difficult for John to describe what he saw in the vision. Nevertheless, the horror of the judgment is clear.

From the shaft will come "locusts" (vv. 6-11) that are no ordinary insects. They will come straight from Satan's domain. They seem to be animal creatures *like* locusts, but they are demonic in nature. Perhaps they are demons who take on the form of these unique locusts, and who are directed by the king of the shaft of the abyss (v. 11).

These locusts inflict a bite like a scorpion's. "The pain from the sting of a scorpion, though not generally fatal, is, perhaps, the intensest that any animal can inflict upon the human body. The insect itself is the most irascible and malignant that lives, and its poison is like itself. . . It is also difficult to guard aginst them, if they can be warded off at all, because they fly where they please, dart through the air, and dwell in darkness" (J.A. Seiss, *The Apocalypse*, Zondervan, p. 83). Unlike ordinary locusts, these creatures will not attack vegetation, but only men. They will be released for five months, during which time men will be unable to commit suicide. This seems impossible, but somehow it will be so.

It is difficult for us to imagine such creatures, but this is no reason for thinking they are mere symbols. Remember that the power of Satan and his demons is great—and these ferocious locusts are demonic. Little wonder that this is called the first *woe*. Since men do not believe in or accept the existence and activity of demons, people then alive will probably try to give some natural explanation for these creatures, and will try to destroy them with a hastily concocted pesticide. But they will find no explanation, and their antidotes will not work.

The Second Woe—the Sixth Trumpet Judgment (Rev. 9:13-21). Under the fourth seal judgment, one fourth the population of the earth will be killed; under the sixth trumpet judgment, an additional one-third will die. This means that these two judgments alone will reduce the population of the earth by one half. Add to this all those who will be killed through war, famine, and disease, and it is not difficult to see how common death will be during this awful time.

The means of this judgment will be an army of horsemen numbering 200 million. Many understand these troops to be the armies of the Orient as they march to invade Palestine. Others see them as a horde of demons, for Scripture gives other examples of supernatural armies (2 Kings 2:11; 6:13-17; Rev. 19:14). The weapons of destruction here will be fire, smoke, and brimstone (9:17). Since these are weapons of hell, they perhaps indicate that this army is made up of demons, the inhabitants of hell.

One would think that the long obituary columns in the newspapers would startle men into facing their responsibility toward God. Instead of repenting and turning to Him for mercy, however, those who are not killed by this army will harden their hearts. The religion of unsaved men during the Tribulation will be the worship of demons and idols, and murder, sorcery, fornication, and stealing will be common (vv. 20-21). Sorcery may include the misuse of drugs, for we derive the word *pharmacy* from the Greek term. It is interesting to notice that three of these four practices are direct violations of the Ten Commandments. Man's ethics will be a reflection of his religion, and during those days vice, rather than virtue, will reign triumphant.

The Third Woe—the Seventh Trumpet Judgment (Rev. 11:15-19). With the sounding of the seventh trumpet will come the announcement that the end is at hand, though seven other judgments must be poured on the earth before all will be finished. These judgments will be the bowls of the wrath of God (16:1-21). These last plagues will come in the closing months, or possibly even weeks, of the last year of the Tribulation, without interruption or pause. The seven angels that have to do with these last judgments will all be told to pour out their judgments at one time. All this will be happening at the same time that Antichrist demands that men worship him. Men will be pressured from every side. Most will decide to cast their lot with Antichrist.

The Seven Bowls

The First Bowl Judgment (Rev. 16:2) will bring on men a grievous sore described as "bad and evil." These words could mean malignant and indicate some sort of cancer. This affliction will come only on those who worship the beast, believers being exempt. But apparently the beast will be able to do nothing for his followers, for they will continue to curse God for these sores even after the fifth bowl has been poured out (v. 11).

The Second Bowl Judgment (Rev. 16:3) will turn the waters into blood. Every living thing in the sea will die. The rather vivid phrase pictures ships wallowing in blood. Under the second trumpet judgment, a third of the sea creatures died (8:9), now the destruction of marine life will be total. Can you imagine the stench and disease this will bring to people who live along the seashores of the world? Seventy-two percent of earth's surface is water.

The Third Bowl Judgment (Rev. 16:4-7), like the third trumpet judgment, will affect the fresh water supply so that it will become blood. The victims of this plague will experience inexorable retribution. They will have shed the blood of the saints and prophets, so now they will have to drink blood. They will deserve what they receive. It is not easy for us to conceive of God dealing with people in this manner. For thousands of years He has been long-suffering and gracious, not dispensing the kind of judgment the world deserves.

The Fourth Bowl Judgment (Rev. 16:8-9) will find the strength of the sun so heightened that it will scorch men with intense heat. Once again, men will harden their hearts instead of turning to God in repentance.

The Fifth Bowl Judgment (Rev. 16:10-11) will affect the throne of the beast and will darken his capital. This will likely slow down his attempt to force all men to worship him. The result will be that men will gnaw their tongues and blaspheme God for their pains and sores, for pain always seems worse in darkness than in the light.

The Sixth Bowl Judgment (Rev. 16:12-16) will dry up the Euphrates River (which previously will have been turned into blood). This will facilitate the crossing of the river by the armies of the kings of the East (Dan. 11:44) as they rush to the Battle of Armageddon.

The Seventh Bowl Judgment (Rev. 16:17-21) will bring widespread destruction and havoc, and with it will be heard the cry, "It is done!" Many physical disturbances will follow. An earthquake will divide Jerusalem and cause other cities to fall. Islands and mountains will disappear, and there will be an unheard-of storm in which single hailstones will weigh 100 pounds. But in spite of the severity and universality of these last judgments, men who survive them will persist in blaspheming God rather than turn to Him for mercy. Everything that man has built in this world will literally collapse before his very eyes, yet he will think he is still the master of his fate and that he has no need for God.

The conclusion of this judgment will bring men to the end of the Tribulation and to the Second Coming of Christ to begin His reign over earth. Only one more part of the picture remains to be completed.

Unbelievable but Inevitable

To review: before the middle of the Tribulation, the western ruler, Antichrist (the man of sin), keeping his treaty with Israel, will invade and conquer Egypt. At that point the Russian armies form the north will invade and overrun Palestine, and when all appears hopeless for both Antichrist and Israel, God will step in and supernaturally destroy Russia's northern armies. This will give the man of sin a free hand to break his covenant with Israel, set himself up to be worshiped, and try to conquer the world.

As he proceeds with his program, however, the nations of the

Orient will unite and attempt to stop him. To do this, they will march west into Palestine. The sixth bowl judgment will dry up the Euphrates River, speeding their entry into the Promised Land. In the meantime, Antichrist will have planted himself firmly in Palestine as a religious and political ruler.

The battlefield in which the armies from east and west will meet will be the plain of Esdraelon, the area around the mountains of Megiddo. That's why the battle is called Armageddon—*Ar* meaning mountain. This plain is about 20 miles south-southeast of Haifa, and the valley today is about 20 miles by 14. By the end of the Tribulation, much of earth's topography will have been changed, and though the battle will center in Megiddo, it will extend some 50 miles to Jerusalem (Rev. 14:20; Zech. 14:2).

In the midst of the battle, the Lord Jesus Christ will return, and the armies of heaven will conquer the armies of earth (Rev. 19:11-21). The carnage will be unbelievable, though the description of it (14:20; 19:17-18) may well be hyperbolic.

But the outcome is certain—the beast will be defeated and his armies captured. He and his false prophet-lieutenant will be thrown into the lake of fire to be tormented forever. Thus the Tribulation will close.

Why must there be such a time as this? There are at least two reasons: first, the wickedness of man must be punished. God may seem to be doing nothing about evil now, but someday He will act. A second reason is that man must, by one means or another, be prostrated before the King of kings and Lord of lords. He may do so voluntarily now by coming to Christ in faith and receiving salvation. Later he will *have* to do so, receiving only condemnation.

These will be the next seven years after the Rapture. Unbelievable? Remember, all other prophecies of the Bible have come to pass. These will too.

10
Peace on Earth

"Peace on earth, good will toward men" is the tantalizing prize men have sought ever since it was first announced by angels at the time of Christ's birth. But many men have failed to understand that God did not promise that peace would follow the Lord's *first* coming. Rather, it will come after His *second* coming.

Individual peace with God, through faith in Christ, is a result of Christ's first coming into this world; but *universal* peace will result only from His second coming. After He returns, the world will experience universal peace for a time period known as the Millennium (Latin for "thousand years"), and then forever in the eternal state.

Clearing the Way

After the Lord returns and defeats His enemies in the midst of the battle of Armageddon, certain judgments will prepare the way for the setting up of Christ's kingdom.

1. All Jews who survive the Tribulation will be judged (Ezek. 20:34-38). This judgment will prevent any rebels from enjoying the millennial reign. The Lord spoke of this judgment in parable form (Matt. 25:14-30), and in the Olivet discourse placed it immediately after His return and the full regathering of the Jewish people (24:30-31; 25:6).

The result of this judgment will be that the unsaved will be cut off from both millennial and eternal life (Ezek. 20:37; Matt. 25:30), and that the redeemed will enter the kingdom of their earthly bodies.

2. There will also be a judgment on Gentiles who will have lived

through the Tribulation. The time of this judgment is clearly specified (Matt. 25:31-46) as "when the Son of man shall come in His glory." It will take place on the earth in what is called "the valley of Jehoshaphat" (Joel 3:2). This will perhaps be a valley that is created in the Jerusalem area by some of the physical disruptions connected with the Second Coming (Zech. 14:4). The people involved in this judgment are "the nations," a Hebrew term translated "people," "heathen," "nations," and, most often, "Gentiles." Since this seems to be an individual judgment, rather than one of national groups, it would probably be best to translate it "Gentiles."

The basis of judging will be the treatment by these Gentiles of a group which Jesus called "My brethren" (Matt. 25:40). Who are Jesus' "brethren"? The answer may be determined by elimination. Since Christ is present as Judge, and the church has been raptured, and living Gentiles are *being* judged, the only group left would seem to be the Jews of the Tribulation.

We have already been introduced to a large group of Jews who will be special messengers of truth in the Tribulation (the 144,000 of Rev. 7). These and others will be objects of intense persecution. Anyone who befriends them or does any act of kindness toward them will himself come under great suspicion. No one will feed, clothe, or visit these Jews simply for humanitarian reasons. To do the things mentioned (Matt. 25:35-36) will involve a real risk of life; doing those things will therefore be evidence of new life in the doer's heart. In other words, the works of kindness which these Gentiles will have done for the Jewish brethren of the Lord will prove the regenerated condition of these Gentiles. The brethren, then, according to this interpretation, are evidently the believing witnesses of the Tribulation, and the basis of judgment will be the works of these individual Gentiles as manifestations of the presence of Christ in their hearts.

As a result of this judgment, those whose lives give evidence of the new birth will become citizens of the kingdom (v. 34). On the other hand, those whose works proved their lack of eternal life will be consigned to the lake of fire (v. 41). Those who enter the kingdom will apparently enter with their earthly bodies, as did the living Jews who successfully passed through the previous judgment. People like these will of course continue to marry and bear children; they account for the population of the earth over whom Christ will rule in the Millennium.

3. There will also be a judgment on Satan before the kingdom is finally set up (Rev. 20:1-3). An angel who has a chain and the key to the bottomless pit will be the agent of this judgment. The devil will be bound, cast into the abyss, and sealed inside it. Language could hardly be more expressive of the totality of his confinement. Its purpose will be to prevent his deceiving the nations during the thousand years of the kingdom. Satan is not bound now, but is loose to deceive the nations and even believers. Otherwise, why would we be exhorted to resist him and to be alert to his devices? *Believers* may overcome Satan today, but he is still "on the loose" and active.

There are the three judgments, at the Second Coming of Christ, that will make way for the setting up of the kingdom. Two other judgments, not related to any particular feature of the kingdom, will also occur. There is difference of opinion as to when Old Testament believers will be raised and judged, but some believe this will take place at the Second Coming of Christ rather than at the Rapture. The New Testament is not explicit on this point, though the Old Testament seems to place the event at the time of the Second Coming (Dan. 12:1-2). Those raised Old Testament believers will be given resurrection bodies and will take their place in heaven with members of the church, the body of Christ.

At this same time, the saints of the Tribulation who did *not* survive the persecution and judgments will be raised and judged. John saw this group in his vision and recorded their resurrection (Rev. 20:4). These, too, like the Old Testament believers, will be given resurrection bodies. They will share in Christ's millennial rule rather than be as those who will be living on earth in ordinary bodies under the divine government.

Government by God

The millennial government will, of course, be set up on this earth. "The Lord shall be King over all the earth: in that day shall there be one Lord, and His name one" (Zech. 14:9). The topography of the earth will have been changed by the time the kingdom is functioning, and the city of Jerusalem, not New York or London, will be the center of all the world government (Isa. 2:3). That city will be exalted (Zech. 14:10); she will be a place of great glory (Isa. 24:23); the site of the temple (Isa. 33:20); and the joy of the whole earth (Ps. 48:2). Jerusalem, scene of so much present dispute and victim of future judgments in the Tribulation, will never again need to fear for her safety (Isa. 26:1-4). "The earth shall be full of the knowledge of the Lord, as the waters cover the sea" (Isa. 11:9). News media of the Millennium will carry Jerusalem datelines for many of their stories.

The Lord Jesus will reign in the millennial theocracy. God used the theocratic form of government for Israel in Old Testament times, but the people demanded a human king. This time, in the theocracy, Christ will reign over the affairs of men. He will fulfill forever the promises God made to David.

As King, Christ will rule all the earth (Dan. 7:14), and the result will be perfect and complete justice for all His subjects. He will punish sin without question (Isa. 11:4; 65:20).

God promises that Christ "shall not judge after the sight of His eyes, neither reprove after the hearing of His ears: but with righteousness shall He judge the poor, and reprove with equity for the meek of the earth: and He shall smite the earth with the rod of His mouth, and with the breath of His lips shall He slay the wicked. And righteousness shall be the girdle of His loins, and faithfulness the girdle of His reins" (Isa. 11:3-5).

Here is the secret of peace on earth—a ruler who can enforce peace righteously.

Do you realize that the Lord may use David, among others, as a regent? A number of prophecies speak of David's important place in the millennial rule (Jer. 30:9; Ezek. 37:24-25). Apparently David, who with other Old Testament believers will be resurrected at the Second Coming of Christ, will act as a prince under the authority of the King. Others will also share in carrying out governmental functions.

Authority over the 12 tribes of Israel will be vested in the hands of the 12 Apostles (Matt. 19:28). Other princes and nobles will likewise share in government duties (Jer. 30:21; Isa. 32:1). It seems, too, that many lesser people will have responsibilities in various departments of the millennial government. The parable of the pounds (Luke 19:11-27) indicates that those who have proved their faithfulness will be given more authority. The church, too, will share in governing the earth (Rev. 5:10). Many of the normal procedures of the millennial government will be carried out by subordinates, but all will be subject to the King of kings and Lord of lords.

The subjects of the rule of Christ during the kingdom will be the Jews and Gentiles who survive the Tribulation and enter the Millennium in earthly bodies. It would appear that at the beginning, then, there will be not a single unsaved person in the kingdom. Nevertheless, it will not be long before a baby is born, then another and another, until in the first 15 or 20 years, there will be a large number of teenagers in the kingdom. Some of them will have accepted Christ as Saviour and some will not. But all who live in this period must accept, outwardly at least, the authority of the King, or else they will be punished with even physical death. Outward allegiance will be required, but many will also give the King heart-allegiance. These people will have mortal bodies similar to ours today. Those who, like the church, have resurrection bodies, will not be subject to physical limitations. Nor will they contribute to space, food, or governmental problems during the Millennium. On the contrary, they will share in Christ's righteous rule.

Earthly, but Spiritual Too

It is sometimes thought that the kingdom cannot be spiritual in character because it is also earthly, but there need to be no contradiction between "earthly" and "spiritual." If the two were incompatible, Christians today couldn't be expected to live spiritual lives. Actually, during the Millennium God will join the spiritual and the earthly in a final display of His glory on this earth. The kingdom will manifest the highest standards of spirituality.

We have already noticed features of the kingdom. Righteousness will flourish (Isa. 11:3-5) and peace will be universal (Isa. 2:4). Joy will prevail and the Holy Spirit will be manifest in unusual ways (Isa. 61:3; Joel 2:28-29). Above all, Satan will be bound.

Will the temple be rebuilt for worship with animal sacrifices during the Millennium? This is a question over which expositors are divided. Ezekiel 40—46 would seem to prophesy these things. Those who do not favor a literal interpretation of this section ask, "Why will sacrifices be needed when Christ is present?" Perhaps the answer to that question eludes us only because we do not fully understand all that will be involved in Millennial worship.

No More Social Injustice

The utopian state which men have dreamed of setting up through politics, spending, and legislation will exist during the Millennium. Success will be assured because Christ will rule the nations with a rod of iron in accord with perfect righteousness and justice (Rev. 19:15), not according to the imperfect desires of the majority. Then, too, many hearts will have experienced the new birth, and this will eliminate the sin question—something which leaders today fail to recognize as man's deepest problem.

The rule of justice will have important ramifications. No longer will courts depend on the usual avenues of evidence—the eyes and the ears—which are subject to error. Instead, Christ will judge accurately on the basis of His complete knowledge of everything (Isa. 11:3-5). No crime will go unpunished; oppression will not be allowed to continue; costs for law enforcement will be cut drastically, thus reducing taxes; and world peace will eliminate military expenditures.

The productivity of the earth will be greatly increased. Isaiah predicted that "the wilderness and the solitary place shall be glad for them; and the desert shall rejoice, and blossom as the rose. It shall blossom abundantly, and rejoice even with joy and singing: the glory of Lebanon shall be given unto it, the excellency of Carmel and Sharon; they shall see the glory of the Lord, and the excellency of our God" (Isa. 35:1-2). The curse, to which earth was subjected (Gen. 3:17) after the sin of Adam, will be reversed, though it will not be completely lifted until the end of the Millennium, when death is finally vanquished. Increased rainfall, food, and productivity will bring in an era of great prosperity for all, and the rule of justice will guarantee that all are properly paid for whatever they produce by way of products or services. Peace on earth will also mean prosperity on earth.

In addition, physical life will be lengthened so that a 100-year-old person will be considered still a youth (Isa. 65:20), and in every way life will be better than it had ever been since sin came into man's history.

The Last Rebellion

You and I may be tempted by the world, the flesh (the sin nature within us), or the devil. During the Millennium, the devil will be bound and out of operation. The world will be so greatly changed that it will have lost much of its power as an evil system that opposes God. But the sin nature will still exist in the lives of unsaved people. We have already seen that even though all who enter the Millennium will have been redeemed, babies will be born, from the first day on, who may or may not experience the saving grace of Christ. All people will be obliged to give outward allegiance to Christ, but, as in every age, Christ will not *compel* men to receive Him as personal Saviour. Consequently, many living at the end of the thousand years will not have trusted Christ for salvation, even though they will have obeyed Him as the Head of the government. The will to rebel will be present within these people as long as they have to live under Christ's rule, for unsaved men are and always will be at enmity against God (Rom.

8:7). But an opportunity to revolt will not come until a leader appears in the person of Satan, who will be released from the abyss for a short season at the end of the Millennium.

As soon as Satan has been loosed, he will deceive the nations again just as he did before and he will be successful, as has often been true. His influence will be worldwide, affecting "the nations which are in the four quarters of the earth" (Rev. 20:8), and his purpose will be to lead men in open, violent revolution against Christ.

The nations which follow Satan are further identified as Gog and Magog (Rev. 20:8). However, this revolution is not the battle described in Ezekiel 38—39. Here the terms seem to be used in a wider sense, meaning a ruler (Gog) and the people (Magog). In the battle described by Ezekiel, the reference to Gog and Magog is limited to people from the north of Palestine—perhaps from Russia; in the Revelation the term includes all nations of earth. The Ezekiel battle will occur during the Tribulation; this one at the end of the Millennium. The army described in Ezekiel will be buried in Israel; this one will be devoured by fire from heaven. The two battles are different in several important respects.

The last revolution will perhaps shape up somewhat as follows: Satan, after his release, will deceive some of the sub-rulers who had been working in the millennial government. Many will respond to his incitement to revolt. Armies will be formed and the revolution will gather momentum as the rebellious forces head for the capital city, Jerusalem, to strike at the very center of Christ's government. Just when they are poised for attack, God will send fire from heaven to destroy them completely. That will end forever opposition of any kind to the Lord God and to Christ.

Why will God permit this last revolution? Obviously, He *must* permit it; otherwise Satan would not be loosed, the revolt would never be allowed to spread, and the armies could never get as far as Jerusalem before being destroyed. God, in allowing this last revolt, will prove two important facts:

1. He will show that a perfect environment, such as the

Millennium will provide in the physical, economic, and social realms, will not change men's hearts. Betterment is not the same as conversion.

2. He will show that universal knowledge of God in the world is not the same as personal knowledge of God in the heart. Men's hearts can be changed only by a supernatural act of grace, not by knowledge or social betterment. But men, even to the end of time, will never learn this lesson, as this last revolution proves conclusively.

The people who joined this revolt will be destroyed by fire. Their leader, Satan, will be cast into the lake of fire (Rev. 20:10). These people will be raised and judged immediately, at the Great White Throne, and will then also be sent into the lake of fire.

Death is not annihilation; Satan, the beast, the false prophet, and all the unsaved, will be tormented in the lake of fire forever. It is not possible to state more emphatically than in verse 10 that this punishment is *eternal*. If it is not eternal, then neither is God—nor eternal life. The same terminology is used of all three (1 Tim. 1:17; Matt. 25:46).

Final Judgment (Rev. 20:11-15)

At the conclusion of Satan's last revolt, a great white throne will be established in space, for the present earth and the starry heavens will have been replaced. The Judge who will sit on this throne will be Christ (John 5:22). Those who appear in this judgment will be the unsaved dead of all time. All the redeemed will have been previously raised (Rev. 20:6) and been previously judged.

The wicked dead will be judged on the basis of their works (vv. 12-13). When the Book of Life is opened, it will be seen that no name of anyone standing before the throne appears in it. Rejection of the Saviour, apparently, excludes men's names from the Book of Life. The works that these men have done in life, as recorded in God's record books (v. 12), will prove on their own terms that they deserve eternal punishment.

It is almost an act of condescension, on God's part, to show men, at this judgment, that on the basis of their personal records they deserve the lake of fire. Some also feel that judging men on the basis of their individual works will be the basis for different degrees of punishment in hell (Luke 12:47-48).

For all who face this judgment, the result will be the same—they will be cast into the lake of fire. This is the second death—eternal separation from God. Even death (which claims the body) and Hades (which claims the soul) will be cast into the lake of fire, for their work will be finished. Death will be conquered forever. Time will be at an end. Eternity will begin.

So What?

Before placing the final period at the end of the last sentence, I want to remind you that you should have two important reactions to this study:

1. Never for a moment doubt the truth and accuracy of the prophecies of the Word of God. There are many details about which we cannot be dogmatic, but the outline of things to come is perfectly clear in the Scriptures. Don't worry about what you can't understand, but be concerned about what you *do* understand about the future. The routine and normalcy of life can easily lull you into the sleep of disbelieving that these things will come to pass in our world.

2. Knowledge must affect life. One cannot know these prophecies and live in the world of the 20th century without feeling keenly that these events will begin to happen shortly. And this ought to affect the way you live from day to day. Peter put it this way: "Seeing then that all these things shall be dissolved, what manner of persons ought ye to be in all holy conversation and godliness? . . . Wherefore, beloved, seeing that ye look for such things, be diligent that ye may be found of Him in peace, without spot, and blameless" (2 Peter 3:11, 14).

The success of your study will be measured by the godliness of your life. May you always be an "A" student of prophecy!